WHEN THE SOUL SHINES

Samar Al-Samaraiy

Copyright © *Samar Al-Samaraiy*, 2025
All Rights Reserved

This book is subject to the condition that no part of this book is to be reproduced, transmitted in any form or means; electronic or mechanical, stored in a retrieval system, photocopied, recorded, scanned, or otherwise. Any of these actions require the proper written permission of the author.

Table of Contents

Dedication 1

Chapter One The Cafe And The Last Encounter 3

Chapter Two 7

Chapter Three.. 12

Chapter Four 19

Chapter Five 29

Chapter Six 34

Chapter Seven.. 43

Chapter Eight 51

Chapter Nine 59

Chapter Ten 64

Chapter Eleven... 73

Chapter Twelve.. 80

Chapter Thirteen.. 92

Chapter Fourteen 100

Chapter Fifteen 113

Chapter Sixteen 119

Chapter Seventeen 125

Chapter Eighteen 135

Chapter Nineteen... 145

Chapter Twenty 156

Chapter Twenty-One... 165

Chapter Twenty-Two... 174

Dedication

To the souls who believed their time had passed, life forever holds a new beginning for those who dare to rise again.

We all yearn...

There's no cure for nostalgia.

Even our imaginary journeys are only fleeting painkillers. Then nostalgia returns, wounding wider, gnawing at what little remains of our patience with ferocious silence. We laugh, we frolic, but the nostalgia before bedtime has an irresistible flavor, sneaking in stealthily, awakening in the heart an unquenchable pain...

Chapter One

The Cafe and the Last Encounter

There are places we visit not only with our feet, but also with our memories, hearts, and the everlasting past that stays with us.

On the banks of the Tigris, morning was quietly dawning, with the sun's golden rays gently touching the water's surface, as if playing a silent symphony heard only by those who love the river and are used to its silence. Seagulls squawked and danced on the edges of the waves, while sparrows twittered above the tree branches, as if participating in nature's sacred harmony.

Amidst this captivating scene, Nahla sat in the old café near the boat dock on the Adhamiya Corniche. The walls, wood, and fragrance preserved the nectar of the most beautiful days of her life. The place bore witness to her laughter and her companions, Howayda and Alaa, and was also the cradle of her immortal love story with her martyred fiancé, Nidal, hat tale woven by time with transparent threads of longing and dreams.

She was waiting for her two lifelong friends to bid them farewell before leaving Baghdad for the United Arab Emirates, after her family decided to emigrate in 1995.

Her hand spontaneously reached for the coffee cup in front of her, made of blue-painted porcelain, in which orange danced like the Baghdad sunset, surrounded by a delicate golden rim, gleaming quietly under the sunlight filtering through the window. She raised it to her lips, the heat of the cup gently spreading through her fingertips, as if she were touching the warmth of memories that had not yet cooled. The steam rising from the spout of the cup twisted like a shy oriental dance, carrying with it the scent of roasted coffee, mixed with the smell of the river and longing.

She lifted a lock of her chestnut hair that had fallen over her face and took her first sip. The coffee tasted bitter, but it flowed smoothly down her throat, resembling the days that had passed in her life; days that melted between sweetness and bitterness, between hope and defeat. She looked at the bottom of the cup, and the small black vortex the coffee had left, as if she were reading a mysterious future in it, or searching for Nidal's face in the lines of the coffee. The cup was not just a vessel, but a companion for hours of contemplation and waiting, and a mirror for the memories she had gathered in this corner that carried the scent of a past that would not return.

She placed the cup quietly on the wooden table, covered with the marks of old cups, and was overcome by a fleeting sense of serenity that faded with each sip, just as days fade without struggle, without a promise, without a conclusion. Nahla, in her thirties, was slender, with a tanned complexion and medium-length hazel eyes resembling the rays of the sun, with distinct oriental features. On this important day in her life, she wore a black skirt that almost touched her ankles and a sun-patterned dress that reflected the radiance of her face.

While she was lost in the whirl of memories, she was alerted to the sound of familiar footsteps, footsteps that carried with them a piece of her heart and a piece of her past. Alaa and Howayda arrived. The arrival of the two friends interrupted Nahla's moment of reminiscing, as if time had taken her back to when they used to meet in the same corner, at the same table.

Howayda stepped forward with her usual lightheartedness and said jokingly:

"Oh, Nahla... you're still in the same corner, as if time hadn't passed." Alaa interrupted her with a different, loving opinion:

"My dear Howayda, who has no beginning can have no end. This corner, with its table and chairs, is not just a place for Nahla, but the history of us all."

Nahla laughed and reached out to hold their hands:

"How I'll miss being provoked like that... I pray to God never to separate us." Howaida said decisively:

"It's impossible for you to escape from us. It's only a 45-minute flight, and I'll be with you in the Emirates. Have you forgotten that I live in Riyadh?"

Alaa added a hopeful smile on her face:

"And don't forget, I'm coming back in two months. We'll meet and continue meeting no matter what."

Howaida continued enthusiastically, as if she wanted to make an unbreakable promise: "My dear, we have not and will not part ways. Let's pledge from now on to continue meeting no matter how far apart we are."

As they ate hot pastries with tea, Howaida noticed something and asked, genuinely curious:

"Nahla, how did your family come up with the idea of traveling? You completed the procedures in record time. What, I wonder, was the motive for emigrating?"

Nahla sighed, stared into space for a moment, then said:

"The blockade on Iraq, as you know, has made life very difficult, so my sister Adhraa and my brother Ayad decided that we must all leave. Even though I don't want to leave Baghdad, I..."

She paused for a moment, then murmured with deep faith: "Whatever God chooses is best."

Alaa nodded, her words sounding like a shared pain:

"Indeed... I am no longer able to fulfill my children's and husband's obligations. Although he is an engineer and works in a government department, his salary is barely enough for us and does not give him the dues he deserves as an engineer. So, we too have decided to immigrate to the UAE. My husband has secured a good job contract, and we will leave, God willing, in two months so we can enroll our children in school."

It was a warm, intimate meeting in which they shared memories and hopes. When it came to an end, they exchanged kisses and said goodbye. Nahla felt as if she was leaving behind a part of her soul in this place. She bid them farewell with a smile and a tear, but deep down, she knew that if the next meeting took place, it would not be the same... and perhaps one day they would meet in another café, overlooking not the Tigris, but the sea... in the land of exile.

As she returned home, she bid farewell to the streets, whispering to herself:

Some places never leave the soul, even if the distances grow far, for the hearts that we knew with sincerity remain close, no matter how much life separates us.

Chapter Two

(1)
The Family at the Crossroads of Departure

In bidding farewell to homelands and loved ones, we carry with us the memory so that we do not get lost when we are expatriates.

Nahla returned home in the evening, carrying a mixture of love and longing for her friends. The house was filled with relatives who had come to bid them farewell before their departure. It was a rare opportunity that brought the family together, after her older sister Nadine and her children had been away from Baghdad for more than two years. Jumana and her children were there, and Marwan with his wife and twins, as if they were trying to take one last group photo of the family and their grandchildren, to be etched in their memory. Despite the warm moment, a void remained in their hearts due to the absence of their older brother Omar, who had left the country.

As night approached, most of the relatives dispersed, but the brothers and sisters decided to spend the night at home for a whole week until their departure to the Emirates. Meanwhile, Nahla, her mother, her older sister Adhraa, and her brother Iyad were preparing to travel to the Emirates via Basra and from there to the port of Al-Faw, where the ship that would carry them to Dubai would dock, dreaming of a new beginning.

Amid the hustle and bustle of conversation and laughter, Nahla left the hall and went quietly to her room. She closed the door behind her as if closing the world for a few minutes. She wanted to be alone with herself and express what remained unsaid. She reached into her small drawer and took out her old notebook, that silent friend who had accompanied her for so long and embraced her scattered feelings for years. She opened it slowly, grabbed the pen, and began to write what was raging in her heart.

The first page:

"Today I bid farewell to a part of my life, and many things I loved have now become memories. Even the corner where Howayda, Alaa, and I used to meet will remain there, empty except for our pictures. I feel as if I am putting the past in a small box, carrying it with me to give me strength when I need it.

My dear Nidal, don't think that my departure will leave you forgotten. Rather, you are a part of my soul. Can a person live while uprooting a part of himself?!"

She paused for a moment and smiled faintly. She felt that the words, despite their simplicity, were an accurate echo of what had been rumbling in her heart for a long time. She turned the page and continued writing.

The Second Page:

"Tomorrow, a new chapter in my life will begin. I will write another story, not a replacement for the past, but an extension of it. I hope that my new story will be honorable for me and for all those who love me. The most important thing is that I remain as I have always been. I don't know what fate holds for me, nor what the future will hold for the Emirates, but I believe that every beginning holds good within it, as long as the foundation is solid and faith is steadfast."

Nahla put the pen aside and closed her notebook. She took a deep breath, feeling a sense of relief, as if writing had arranged her scattered thoughts and gently scattered the sadness in the corners of the pages. She sat on the edge of the bed, contemplating the room around her, then looked out the window overlooking the garden, where the gardenia tree she had planted in her youth stood. Its fragrant scent filled the space whenever the breeze blew, like an echo of her childhood. That tree wasn't just a passing plant, but a symbol of continuity and hope, a witness to unforgettable moments. She'll miss its scent, which makes her feel connected to the roots of her first home, even if those days are now just a distant memory.

Outside, the sound of her brothers' laughter filtered in from under the door, like a dim light reassuring her that she was not alone in this journey.

She smiled despite the pang that filled her heart and said to herself:

"The distances may be long, but those who truly love us remain close, no matter how far the geography."

(2)
Between Origin and Destiny

The family is a tree rooted in a single origin, its branches branching out towards different destinies, but it remains connected by the arteries of memory and nostalgia.

Nahla was born the youngest member of a large family living in the Adhamiya neighborhood of Baghdad. The family consisted of four sisters and three brothers.

Her father, may God have mercy on him, was an employee in a vegetable oil factory, while her mother was a skilled seamstress. Despite their parents' care to distribute love equally, Nahla, the youngest of her siblings, always felt that she lived in the shadow of her older siblings, while Jumana, Adhraa, Ayad, and Marwan received double the attention, each for their own reasons.

Her older brother, Omar, could not bear the harshness of life in Iraq and did not complete his studies. He immigrated to Turkey and then settled in Canada, where he married and began a new life away from his family. After him, her second sister, Adhraa, went through tragic circumstances after the death of her husband in a traffic accident, without having any children. She returned to the family home to live in its care once again.

Adhraa was always the second mother in the family, and she took over the support of the family after the death of their father in 1990. She was forced to leave her job as a tour guide after the beginning of the siege and opened a small bookstore selling stationery and magazines, in addition to her work translating documents, with financial support from her younger brother, Ayad.

Nadine, the third sister, tended to rebel. She always felt that she was being financially exploited, and that the family only turned to her when needed. She did not maintain her relationship with anyone except Marwan, who remained the closest to her heart. She lavished money and gifts on him as if he were her only child.

Jumana, the fourth sister, and Ayad, the next in line, were the closest siblings to their mother, especially the eldest sister.

However, Ayad faced marital problems due to this closeness, which led to the collapse of his marriage and his return to the family home after their father's death to share responsibility with Adhraa.

Among them all, Marwan, the sixth brother stands out with his mystery and volatility. His fateful decisions were always surprising, including his absence for eight months working in a petrochemical refinery in Mosul, and his sudden return to Baghdad, with his wife pregnant with twins, without any family members knowing about his marriage. This initially shocked his mother, but she quickly calmed down when she knew that his wife was an engineer from a prominent family.

Despite the siblings' relative stability, the family home was not without tensions. Jumana, despite being married and having three children (two girls and a boy), continued to interfere in family affairs and exploited her mother's love for Adhraa to demand money, believing that Nahla, with her low income, did not deserve support. In her opinion, the high cost of living puts her first, even if her husband owned a house and a car.

Chapter Three

(1)
The Farewell Table... and the Warmth of the Last Picture

What unites us is not the tables we gather around, but the hearts that silently ached at farewells, storing deep within them images that cameras could not capture, but rather that they preserved to remain more faithful than memory.

Early in the morning, the family members woke up to the sound of Marwan calling them to eat the breakfast he had brought from the market. The table was rich. with the most delicious Iraqi dishes (Qaymar with Kahi, Iraqi molasses, stone bread, and meat borek), which added an unforgettable warmth and nostalgia. Everyone, young and old, gathered around the table, exchanging conversations and laughter.

In a spontaneous moment, Ayad surprised them by bringing the camera to take pictures, as an everlasting memory of the last full family gathering before he traveled with his mother and two sisters, Adhraa and Nahla, to the UAE.

The whole family, and Ayad pressed the camera button, and the dim light appeared, documenting the moment. Nahla felt that the photo was not just a family snapshot, but a testament to a great but fragile love, like the intertwined branches of trees that fear the wind and separation.

She said to herself:

"Places and things change, and memories are not enough. Love alone will not keep us together, but maybe, just maybe, it will make our return possible one day."

She smiled at the camera, as if smiling at the future, despite its ambiguity. She felt as if she were capturing the images with the eye of her heart, preserving them in her memory, as if they were pages from the book of her life, striving to immortalize the moment with its small details. She stared at her brothers' faces one by one, thinking to herself:

"I wonder if time will allow us to meet again after so many years!" And what would the meeting be like? Would it be with everyone, or would we all meet separately?

At that moment, she wished time would stop so she could enjoy this time, because it was one of the most genuine moments of love the family had ever known. But deep down, she knew that each person was hiding something in their heart, an unspoken feeling, and perhaps never would be.

On the evening of the day before the departure, the family gathered again around the dinner table. The Iraqi feast was full of delicious food, with the aroma of grilled kebabs filling the air. "Kass bel Lahm" (similar to shawarma) shimmered under the kitchen lights, while crispy "Arouk" bread waited its turn on the table. On the other hand, the distinctive sweetness of "Manna C Salwa", the Iraqi dessert that melts in the mouth with its softness, was served alongside the pistachio baklava, which invites everyone to taste it.

The air was filled with spontaneous laughter and cheerful conversation about the details of the trip, as if they were trying to escape the looming specter of separation. Amidst these moments, Nahla spontaneously turned to Marwan and said with a faint smile:

"My dear brother Marwan... I hope we continue to communicate, and don't forget me." Marwan laughed playfully, his usual smile appearing in moments of humor. "You're dreaming, sweetheart. You know I'm always busy. You'd be lucky if I remembered you."

The place erupted with laughter, but deep within Nahla's soul, a silent pang seeped in. Marwan's laughter concealed something else: perhaps anxiety, or a fear that his absence might become a habit. Nahla tried to keep up with the laughter, but settled for a pale smile, her thoughts lost in the corners of silence.

Nadine was following the situation and trying to ease the pressure. She said with enthusiasm mixed with laughter:

"If you miss Marwan, let me know. I'll book plane tickets for him and his family, and we'll all come to visit you. Maybe Jumana will accompany us too. We'll make it a trip to meet and shop."

Joy filled the place again, but this time with genuine warmth. After dinner, everyone began clearing the table as if they were racing against time, making the most of the last moments of the night by being fully present with one another. They then moved to the living room, where the conversations and laughter continued, as they competed in joking about dividing the furniture in the house, especially between Marwan and Jumana.

Marwan said jokingly, waving his hands:

"I'll take Nahla's sofa set and rocking chair, and leave Jumana with the dining table, chairs, and bookcase."

As Nadine gazed with tender eyes at the small pieces the family had collected over the years, she lifted one of the crystal pieces and said with a nostalgic smile:

"I'll take this crystal and porcelain... so I have something from the family left."

As the hours slipped by, tension began to creep into their hearts.

Dawn approached, and sleep wasn't easy for anyone. Ayad checked his

passports for the tenth time and confirmed the ship's departure time, while Nahla arranged her things with a trembling hand, thinking about everything she might forget. As for Adhraa, she was trying to reassure herself that she hadn't overlooked anything, despite her deep feeling that she had forgotten something important.

As dawn approached, silence fell over the house. Everyone had woken up early, as if sleep had refused to visit them. The sound of the taxi that would take them to the port of Umm Qasr in Basra rang in their imaginations before they heard it in reality.

(2)
The First Pulse of Departure

In every farewell, there is a part of our hearts that remains with those we love and a longing that never leaves us, no matter how long the distances

At the threshold of departure, the family stood to bid farewell to Nahla, Adhraa, Ayad, and their mother, in an embrace in which longing was intertwined with fear of the unknown. The scene was not just an ordinary farewell, but rather a farewell to a chapter in life, a page being turned into the family book, at the end of which a heavy note was written:

"The journey began without the father who left them years ago."

At that moment, the father's absence seemed strongly present, as if his shadow stood with them at the door, silently patting their shoulders.

He reminded them not only of those who would leave him, but also of those who had left and would never return, which made the pain even more painful. Marwan embraced Nahla tenderly and said in his deep voice: "Take care of yourself."

Nahla replied in a low voice, with a subtle tremor:

"You too, don't forget us."

Then she turned to Jumana and hugged her for a long time before placing a light kiss on her forehead, as if entrusting her with responsibility. She said in a low but sincere tone:

"I hope you don't forget me, and that I can always hear your voice."

Jumana responded, trying to lighten the moment with humor mixed with love:

"If you send me a monthly amount or gifts, I certainly won't forget you." Everyone laughed, their laughter rising slightly, as if in a desperate attempt to ease the burden of the lump in their throats.

Nadine added in a strong, confident tone that cut through the cloud of sadness:

"I'm not saying goodbye, but rather, see you soon. I'll visit you after you've settled in, God willing."

They got into the car, and as it moved slowly, Nahla looked out the window, as if trying to memorize the details of the final scene. The family stood at the threshold, waving their hearts before their hands. She saw her mother silently wiping away her tears, while the eyes of Marwan, Jumana, Nadine, and the grandchildren all followed the car until it disappeared from their sight.

Dawn was beginning to break, but those rays didn't dispel the question that had settled in Nahla's mind:

"Will the familiarity that unites us continue as we are today, or will the years scatter us like autumn leaves?"

On the way south, the streets seemed to shrink behind them, as if refusing to say goodbye. The car made its long journey amidst an eerie silence, each lost in their own thoughts, emotions rising with every kilometer they moved away from home, from memories, and from Adhamiya.

Nahla, her mother, Adhraa, and Ayad arrived at the Umm Qasr port in Basra at noon, exhausted from the journey. Especially their mother, who was over 65 and had been quietly dealing with her fragile bones and high blood pressure. Her face was steadfast, as if she concealed a determination hidden in her eyes that supported those around her, despite the silent pain.

The port was teeming with travelers, most of them Iraqi families carrying their bags and hopes, clinging to the prospect of survival in a country burdened by war and blockade. This seaport was the only available outlet for travel after the blockade was eased, and the UAE was one of the few countries to open its doors to Iraqis, making this journey a lifeline.

However, the reality was grim. The port lacked services. There were no decent cafeterias or restaurants to provide relief for weary travelers.

Bathrooms were scarce and unsanitary. The port seemed more geared toward cargo than people. Nevertheless, in the large, crowded lobby, the family found a place to rest.

Ayad went to complete the procedures, stamp the passports and pack the bags, while Nahla brought out the simple food she had prepared on their last morning at home, some carefully wrapped sandwiches. It was a psychological reprieve and a piece of home in this strange crowd.

An hour before sunset, the boarding official announced that two double rooms had been reserved: one for Adhra and Ayad, and the other for Nahla and their mother. This was the first real cruise for all of them, and eeriness pervaded everything: the appearance of the ship, the crowds, the salty air, the sound of the waves, and the silent awe in their eyes. As the sailing whistle sounded, the passengers emerged onto the deck, seeking one last, heart-warming farewell.

Nahla and her family also came out. They stood there, silently looking at the shore, which was gradually receding, as if watching a part of their lives slowly being pulled away in front of them. Nahla cried silently, but her tears streamed down her face as if she were saying goodbye to her childhood, her friends, the smell of baking bread in their house, and the chirping of the birds by the kitchen window.

Although her mother was by her side, holding her hand and gesturing for her to look at the horizon and not back, Nahla felt deeply alone.

She was traveling into the unknown with a part of her family, and her heart was heavy, as if she were alone among the crowds.

Chapter Four

(1)
The Sea's Talk... and the Heart's Talk

Love never dies, but rather resides within us like an invisible shadow, which we carry with us wherever we go, as if the heart only beats with what has been lost.

Everyone returned to the ship's lobby, while Nahla remained alone on the deck, staring at the turbulent waves of the sea. Night had fallen over the water, and darkness was beginning to fall. She was talking to herself, recalling memories that had inhabited her heart and never left her. It was as if the sea, with its waves, had summoned from the depths of her being a past she thought she had left behind, but now she realized that it was still alive inside her, accompanying her in a painful silence that never left her.

She reached out and touched the necklace that hugged her neck, the necklace that was associated with the memory of her beloved and martyred fiancé, Nidal. She began to ask herself in a low voice:

"If I had married Nidal without delaying those two years, I wonder... would we have been able to have a child who carried his features and kept him alive in my heart and memory? Perhaps the pain would have eased, and perhaps... instead of losing him, I would have seen him every day in our child's eyes."

Her memory delved back to that distant moment in 1982 when her mother rejected her engagement to Nidal, claiming she was too young for marriage. Nahla was eighteen at the time, and that shock was like a stab in her tender heart, leaving a deep, unhealed wound. After completing her studies at the Institute of Management two years after graduating from high school in 1985, she was finally able to convince her family to accept Nidal as her fiancé. At that moment, their shared dreams began to take shape and appeared before them as if they were within reach.

But just one month after announcing their engagement, Nidal was forced to travel abroad for a year-long training course. This trip was the primary reason their marriage was postponed. When he returned a year later in 1986, the two began planning to build and furnish their home, building their future stone by stone, with hope upon hope. But fate stood in their way, and the death of his father was another reason to postpone their plans for another year.

On a special day in late 1987, they met in the old café on the banks of the Tigris River in Adhamiya Corniche. This was a place that had always witnessed their encounters and silently told their love stories. These were unforgettable moments when Nidal clasped her hands in his and said to her in a calm, hopeful tone:

"Tomorrow, God willing, we will begin digging the foundation for our home, Nahla, just as we planned together… We will have our own home, a home unlike any other."

Nahla smiled as she imagined the happy life she had always dreamed of and responded with hope:

"I know you will, Nidal… and nothing will ever separate us." He returned to her warm smile and said tenderly:

"We will do it together, Nahla. This is the life we are building with our own hands, not anyone else's."

After a few moments of silence, she looked at him with eyes filled with love and said:

"You know, there is a feeling inside me that I've never told you about before."

He looked at her questioningly with a smile: "Since when have you been hiding this from me?"

She raised her gaze to the sky as if gathering her thoughts, then looked back at him and whispered:

"Since the day we first met, every time you said goodbye to me to join the front, I clutched my heart and murmured a prayer for your quick return. I was afraid, and I always had a feeling that our meeting might be our last... I hate goodbyes, Nidal."

Nidal laughed, trying to ease her tension, and said gently:

"Don't worry, my sweetheart." If I am not with you in this world, I will be with you in the afterlife... I am your soul that never leaves you."

Her eyes filled with sadness as she said in a slightly raised voice:

"Please don't mention the afterlife. I know that Allah's promise is true, but your talk about it scares me even more. And I, too, have a promise to myself: If I am not with you in this world, I will never be with anyone else."

Nidal tried to lighten the sad mood, saying, laughing:

"Do you remember Abdel Halim Hafez's song 'Asmar Ya Asmarani'? When we first met, I used to tease you, 'Asmar Ya Asmarani, turn your face to me.' You were extremely nervous, yet you couldn't hold back your laughter."

They laughed together, reminiscing about their early days and how their first encounters were filled with irony and adventure, especially when Nahla was still a high school student. At the end of the meeting, he told her he would be busy in the coming days, taking advantage of his vacation to supervise construction workers as he began digging the foundation for their home.

A week later, Nidal's vacation ended, and he had to return to the front lines in Basra. As usual, he went to see her to bid farewell before his departure on a cold day in February 1988. She held him in her eyes for the last time, bidding him farewell on the threshold of her demise, unaware that Al-Faw would be his final stop and that his soul would be buried there, beyond a border that knew no return. Nahla poured water behind him, as she always did, wishing him well, and said:

"Come back to me safely, Nidal... I will be waiting for you every moment."

Nidal took her hand in his, looked into her hazel eyes with a smile full of tenderness and strength, then kissed her forehead and whispered:

"I will return, Nahla, and I will fulfill all my promises to you. Nothing will separate us, my love, except death."

His words remained engraved in her heart, as if she could hear his voice in every wave and see his face in every drop of water surrounding her on the deck of the ship. She would always place her hand on her heart and murmur:

"The letters of your name are engraved in my heart; neither fear nor separation can erase them".

Nahla overlooked the time until her brother Ayad called her to go down to the restaurant for dinner with the family. She wished to remain immersed in her memories, without anyone interrupting her, as the atmosphere surrounding her encouraged her to recall the most beautiful moments of her life. After dinner, Nahla and her mother returned to their room to rest from the fatigue of the travel and the long wait at the port, and she fell into a deep sleep.

(2)
Heart of Gold

There are souls that, no matter how far away, remain close, inhabiting our breaths and pulsating within us with memories that time does not extinguish.

Nahla woke up before sunrise, prayed the dawn prayer, then quietly went up to the deck of the ship and stood in front of the sea, watching the sun sneak its golden rays from behind the horizon, reflected on the surface of the water, and coloring it with the color of hope. She extended her hands towards the sky, as if she wanted to touch the golden threads of the sun, to weave them into a bracelet to adorn her with the memories of her precious love. She placed her hands on her heart, feeling its pulse, as if she was hearing its whispers telling her about a past that had not left her present.

The image of Nidal passed through her memory, and she said to herself:

"I loved you with a love that makes me see you in everything, in absence and presence, in happiness and fear."

Her memories went back to the day Nidal returned from his travels outside Iraq.

They spent every moment building their home, but their marriage was postponed repeatedly, once because of travel, another time because of his father's death, and then because of his commitment to the front, where the fighting required him to spend extended periods. Despite all the circumstances, Nidal never forgot to make her happy. On every vacation, he brought her a gift. On his last visit before joining the front, he gave her a gold necklace with a heart-shaped medallion in the middle. Each half of the heart bore the letter "N" (the letter "N"), and on the back was engraved the words "I am yours and you are mine."

He told her:

"I asked a jeweler to have it crafted in Basra a month ago, as it would be your birthday while I was at the front. I wanted to be the first to congratulate you. I wanted it to stay with you forever."

Nahla happily put on the necklace, but there was something in her heart heavier than gold. She said to him with a melancholy tone:

"Your name is engraved in my heart, and I don't need a necklace to remind me of you."

Nidal smiled and said confidently:

"I know that... I know that my soul resides in your soul, but I wanted to leave you something of me, even if I'm gone."

Nahla looked at him with eyes full of love and fear, as if she saw in that golden heart hanging around her neck the shadow of the coming separation, as if she realized that that day was the last of her remaining Nedal, alive.

While Nahla was lost in her memories on the deck of the ship, amidst immortal images of Nidal, her mother's voice brought her back to the present, calling her and asking her to join them for breakfast. The air was light and breezy, instilling a sense of serenity in the soul. She joined them for breakfast, which Ayyad had brought to the deck. It was a special breakfast, bringing them together around a table of memories and the tranquility of the sea.

As soon as they finished eating, Adhra escorted their mother to the ship's lobby to sit with the other female passengers, while Ayyad busied himself with new friends he had made. As for Nahla, she preferred to remain on deck. She took a book with her to immerse herself in reading, but the lines could not distance her from the memory of a day that had been a turning point in her life.

Her mind went back to the moments after Nidal joined the Eastern Front. The days were heavy, passing painfully slowly, carrying with them nothing but fear and anticipation. Every night, she waited for news, a message, any sign that would instill hope in her heart. But instead, sad news and mysterious rumors would sneak into her ears, increasing her tension and feeding her fear and anxiety, especially after the battle to liberate Al-Faw on April 17, 1988, in which Nidal and his battalion were achieving victory.

She contacted Nidal's friends who had returned from the front, and they reassured her that he was fine. But contact with his battalion was cut off, and no one could find him. He might have been a prisoner or in an isolated area; no one had an answer. One gray morning, two months after trying to get news of him, on June 17, an officer who was a close friend of Nidal's knocked on the door. Nahla opened the door with fear, almost like numbness. Her eyes met his, a sadness in them that preceded speech. He stood silent, as if time had frozen, then said in a trembling voice that broke the stillness of the moment:

"Nidal... was martyred in the Battle of Al-Faw in the Basra sector. He was buried in enemy territory, in Iran... May God have mercy on him".

Nahla felt the ground shake beneath her feet, and everything around her collapsed.

"Nidal? No... no, impossible. He promised me he'd come back." The officer said, bowing his head in respect and sorrow:

"He was martyred bravely, defending the homeland. He was a hero, Nahla".

She fell to the ground, tears streaming from her eyes as if she had lost the light forever. Everything went out, the colors were lost, the sound was gone, and the universe shrank in her heart. She was transferred to the hospital after collapsing and stayed there for a week, leaving her with a tired body and a soul that refused to believe it. She did not see Nidal, she did not say goodbye to him, and she did not greet his coffin. Her mind was convincing her of his departure, but her heart was still screaming:

"He did not die."

Her internal struggle continued for more than a year. Although she returned to work and resumed her daily life, she was like a robot, a soulless body, living life as nothing more than a duty, her joy stolen from her.

(3)
The Heart Buried Behind Borders

Your martyrdom was a promise to the land, but your heart was a promise to me... and I live in the shadow of both promises.

The years passed heavily, until the day came when fate returned Nidal's body to the homeland, three years after his martyrdom in the prisoner and martyrs exchange agreement in 1991. He returned, carried on the shoulders of men, not as he had left, but he did return. His body was carried like a groom-to-be to be buried in the family cemetery. When Nahla approached the grave, she had collapsed again, dragging the thorns of loss with her feet, her tears preceding her steps. She stood at his grave and extended her trembling hand to stroke the headstone, as if touching his soul, then she whispered:

"Your martyrdom was a promise to the land and the homeland... but your heart was a promise to me. And now I live in the shadow of the two promises. You have returned to me, but you are no longer the same."

She placed her hands on the cold stone and looked at him with the gaze of someone questioning absence:

"You were the dream of my life, the breath I breathe. Today, you dismounted from your horse and left us... but you will remain with me, your spirit shadowing me."

She visits him whenever life feels difficult, holding onto the necklace he had given her, the one with a golden heart in the middle bearing the initial letter of their names, "N." She whispered:

"This heart will remain with me. Until we meet again... You did not die, but you live in me." Her tears were not tears of farewell, but tears of an eternal love that defied death.

The days passed, and Nahla gradually began to heal from the wounds of loss. She did not forget, but she learned to turn memories into energy that illuminated her path through life. She would visit his grave regularly, sit near it, and whisper to him the details of her life as if he could hear her. She would talk to him about her work, her family, and the small dreams that had begun to be given to him. His memory transformed from a pain that tore her apart into a force that propelled her forward. On her last visit before her departure, she stood before the grave, placed one hand on her heart and the other on the headstone, and whispered to him:

"You are with me, Nidal, in every step I take. And I will remain strong for you. Your martyrdom did not take you away from me, but rather made you present in every moment of my life... as if your spirit is watching me from among the clouds."

She returned from that visit carrying a heavy memory, but with a steadfastness that resembled deep silence in her eyes. When her sister called her to join them in the ship's lobby, she hesitated. The deck was her breathing space, and there she felt she was still talking to Nidal, under one sky, one air, and a soul still suspended there, above the waves of life. But she went because life goes on and because she promised him she would be strong... and here she was, fulfilling her promise.

Chapter Five

(1)
Arriving in Dubai

When you leave your homeland, the universe whispers to you that life is broader than the borders of your city, and that your new homeland is made in the hearts of those you love

The family arrived at Port Rashid in Dubai in April 1995 after a two-and-a- half-day sea voyage. Their arrival was not the end of a journey, but rather the beginning of a new life in a land they had never set foot on. They headed directly to Sharjah, where a relative hosted them for two weeks, and then on to Abu Dhabi, where Adhraa began her new job in the stock market.

At first, they rented a furnished hotel apartment. After more than a month of searching, they found a spacious, three-bedroom apartment overlooking the Abu Dhabi Corniche. Its location was ideal, especially since it overlooked the sea. As Nahla often said:

"You never get bored with the sea."

The view of the sea provided them with a sense of tranquility, as if it made up for the harshness of the departure.

Ayad began his job search in Abu Dhabi, wanting to stay close to his mother and two sisters. However, fate led him to work in the emirate of Al Ain, where he found a suitable position. He decided to settle there and visit them on weekends or whenever he could, as the distance between the two cities is only two hours by car.

As for Nahla, she was fortunate to have an outlet for her soul, since this hobby had become part of her work at a center for people with special needs. The salary wasn't large, but it was enough to begin a new chapter where she enjoyed her work. She chose not to leave because its consistent schedule suited her and let her spend more time with her mother. She found sewing and designing children's clothes and abayas to be a true outlet for her soul, as this hobby had stayed with her since she was young. It wasn't just a craft but a lifeline amid storms of longing and sadness.

Despite a difficult start, the family gradually adapted to life in the UAE. The challenges of living abroad were many, but they faced them with steadfastness until they felt a sense of comfort and reassurance. Nahla started her daily routine and worked toward integrating more fully into society. She made friends at work and received indirect support from those around her. She joined a women's sewing and crafts workshop, where her talent began to grow. Her designs for Iraqi abayas and children's clothing gained widespread admiration, and she took part in several local exhibitions. Her creative work became an additional source of income, giving her a sense of independence and hope.

Despite her busy schedule, the most peaceful and relaxing moments of her day were those spent at dawn on the beach. She would sit there, watching the sunrise, and reminisce about her old memories of Baghdad. She whispered to herself:

"The past has become a dream, but an unforgettable dream."

As for now, it was weighing on her soul like a heavy shadow that wouldn't lift. She felt as if she were drowning in a deep sea, and whenever she tried to swim, sadness pulled her back down to the family's restrictions; despite her love for them, they kept her grounded more than they offered her freedom. As she spent her days between work, caring for her mother, and sewing, her heart longed for a moment of breathing that belonged only to her.

(2)
The Spark of Rebellion and the Fateful Decision

Sometimes, breaking free from restrictions is the first step toward finding yourself.

On a sunny summer morning, warm sunlight streamed into Nahla's room as she packed her bags for her trip to Bahrain to participate in a Gulf clothing and perfume exhibition. As she carefully placed the abayas and children's clothes she had expertly designed and sewn, she looked at her plane ticket and entry visa to Bahrain on the bedside table. Her heart was pounding, not only from the excitement of traveling but also from the tension surrounding her decision.

Nahla went to the lounge where her mother was sitting and calmly told her about her travel plans. Her mother responded in a low voice, torn between concern and acceptance, and asked her if she had spoken to Ayad. Nahla sighed and said:

"I told you because you are my mother, and Ayad does not have the right to make decisions for me. I am now forty-eight years old, and I have the right to make my own decisions."

Suddenly, the apartment door opened forcefully, and Ayad entered, his face flushed with anger and his eyes gleaming with fury. He said in an angry voice:

"Nahla, what am I hearing? You're going to travel without consulting me. Who gave you permission?"

Nahla turned slowly and faced him firmly, despite the anxiety and fear that gripped her. She answered him with a calm, collected voice:

"Brother, I've been waiting for this trip for years. This is my chance to participate in a Gulf exhibition. I'll only be away for two weeks. Adhraa will be with my mother, and everything is arranged."

Ayad remained standing like a towering mountain and asked her to bring him the visa. She brought it to him, and he tore it into small pieces, scattering them around the room. Nahla felt as if her heart had been torn apart as well. In a trembling voice, trying to stay still, she said to her brother:

"Ayyad, why are you doing this? This is my chance to get some air. I didn't ask anything of you. This is my right."

With extreme anger, he replied:

"Your right!... Your right is to stay here and consider family above all else. You will not travel, and this decision is final."

Nahla looked at the torn papers on the floor and felt a lump in her throat. Unable to control her tears, they began to flow heavily. She left the living room and went to her room.

Evening fell heavily, and as she sat in her room, the dim lighting revealing a sadness mixed with the pain of her brother and his unfair decisions and her mother's submission to her brother's decisions, she was alone, except for the sound of messages coming to her phone. Among them, one message caught her attention: from her older brother, Omar, who lives in Canada.

She grabbed her phone and quickly dialed, tears streaming down her cheeks.

Omar replied:

"My dear Nahla, how are you?"

With a weary voice and welling up tears, she replied, "I'm not well. I'm tired, Omar. I can't go on. I'm restricted in every way: thought, word, and movement. My actions are being counted against me. I feel disabled and incapable, and they are making decisions for me."

Omar listened to her with longing and said:

"I know you're going through difficult times. I heard what happened to Ayad from my mother, and she asked me to call you to calm you down."

In an encouraging voice, he said to her:

"I called to help you. What do you think about visiting us here in Canada? I'll get you a visitor visa and try to get you a university seat. It's always been your dream to complete your university studies, and you'll definitely have the start of a new life."

Nahla's eyes shone with a faint light of hope. She knew that escaping to Canada might be difficult, but it was the only way for her to break free from the shackles. His words filled her heart with courage. For the first time, she felt there was a path she could take away from all the pressure and control.

Nahla responded, her voice tinged with a faint smile, bitter tears, and a flood of doubt about her ability to stand up again and stabilize her life, saying:

"Do you think that time and space allow me to start over? I'm now forty-eight years old, and soon I'll be fifty!"

Omar answered her with confidence:

"Yes, my sweetheart. Age is not measured by years, but by accomplishments. I am with you in every decision you make. I support you with everything I can do to make you happy."

She ended her call with Omar, filled with joy she hadn't felt in a long time. She whispered to herself:

"Why not? Life begins again when we find someone who extends a hand to us so we can cross over to freedom and hope."

Chapter Six

(1)
The First Step Toward Freedom

Sometimes the hardest decision is the first step toward freedom, but it's also the first step toward the life I deserve

Nahla began to regroup and reorganize her life step by step, intensifying her efforts in sewing to accumulate the capital that would allow her to achieve her goal of traveling to Canada. In addition to the salary she received from the center, with all her attempts to achieve independence, she was confronted with the limitations of her situation due to the interference of Adhraa, Jumana, and Ayad in her life. Even when she considered visiting her friend and life partner, Alaa, in Sharjah, this required Adhraa's approval, on the grounds that she could not leave her mother alone. Therefore, she was forced to set aside the weekend for visits, as Ayad and Adhraa would be with their mother during her absence.

While Jumana, absent yet present, played her usual role of persuading her mother to make decisions that suited her regarding Nahla, Ayad exerted his control over everything related to the household, despite living in another emirate. In addition, everyone was dependent on Adhraa, the family's primary financial provider, which only increased Nahla's sense of being trapped. Amid these restrictions, she clung to her lifelong friends,

Howayda and Alaa, as they were her only refuge and provided her with some peace in this stifling situation.

Throughout two years, Nahla exerted great effort, especially after her success in the field of sewing and her participation in major exhibitions across the Emirates. Her brothers continued to belittle her and increased their pressure on her. She felt like she was swimming against the tide, while her aspirations for a better future became increasingly clear. Although she failed the IELTS English test four times, and in a moment of despair, she decided to give it all up, a voice inside her called out:

"You have to try, you will succeed, and you will prove to everyone that you are strong."

On her fifth attempt at the IELTS exam, she passed and achieved the required score. This in itself was a remarkable success and the beginning of a challenging journey to achieve her set goal. Thus, her dream of independence began to take shape, and she began to implement the idea of immigrating to Canada to begin a new, independent life.

Although this decision was shocking to her family, it was decisive and final for her. With her determination and the support of her older brother, Omar, who remained a constant support, she was able to secure a place at a Canadian university to study for a diploma in "Healthcare and Life Sciences." Omar covered her tuition fees.

At that point, the family had no choice but to submit to Nahla's determination and resolve. Her position was firm and clear, and despite their reservations, they had no choice but to surrender to her decision.

In early April 2015, three months before her scheduled departure for Canada, Nahla received her study visa from a Canadian university in Toronto. For a moment, she couldn't believe what she read: the university had accepted her into the "Healthcare and Life Sciences" diploma program. How could a woman, on the cusp of fifty, have such an opportunity? It seemed like a late dream; a dream carved into the stone of life.

But, as usual, she hid her joy. She didn't dare express it, especially in front of Jumana, Nadine, Adhraa, or even Ayad. She knew very well that joy in this house was met with suspicion and doubt, not with blessing. Jumana, in particular, had been waiting for a moment like this, not to share it, but to extinguish it. On a light spring evening, Nahla decided to confront her mother with the truth.

We sat in the living room. She put her cup of tea aside and looked into her eyes steadily, concealing an invisible inner turmoil. She calmly addressed her mother, saying, "Mom, I received my Canadian study visa today, and I will set a travel date soon."

The mother slowly raised her head; her eyes reflecting astonishment mixed with doubt. She was silent for a long time, then exploded.

"Study! What study? In Canada? When did you apply? Where did you get the money?"

Nahla replied with a confident smile that concealed her trembling heart:

"I spoke with Omar almost a year ago. When he invited me to visit his family, I told him I wanted to study humanities. He was excited, and we began corresponding with universities. When the acceptance letter came from Toronto, they asked for an IELTS certificate. I worked hard and took the exams repeatedly until I got the required score. Omar paid for the first year's tuition to expedite the visa process." As for housing, I covered it on my own: I sold my gold jewelry, saved money from my job, and received my benefits after resigning from the center. And that's how everything worked out, praise be to God."

The mother gripped the edge of the chair, her face taut, her eyes gleaming with hidden anger. She shouted:

"Since when have you been plotting behind my back? Omar hasn't told me anything! And I contact him every day."

Despite her apparent aloofness, Nahla felt an inner turmoil. She whispered to herself:

"Am I really ready for this decision?" But as she recalled the scenes from her past life, certainty returned to her heart. She said to herself, "This is my last chance to develop myself."

She approached her mother, sat on the floor, clasped her hands, and said gently:

"Mom, it wasn't intentional. We just didn't expect the university to accept me at this age."

The anger intensified in the mother's features, and she raised her voice:

"You're fifty years old now. Tell me, for God's sake, what kind of mind are you thinking?" How will you live alone in a cold, distant country? How will you bear responsibility alone?"

Nahla interrupted her with a new sense of awareness:

"And what about Adhraa? Didn't she endure the exile in Malaysia?!"

The mother shouted:

"Don't compare yourself to her. Your sister, Adhra, is smarter and stronger than you, and she was forced to leave."

Suddenly, Nahla exploded with words that had been piling up in her chest for years:

"Of course, I don't resemble Adhra, and I don't want to resemble anyone. In your eyes, I'm nothing, just a servant performing endless duties. When one of my sisters gives birth, I rush to serve her, and you say, 'She's on her own, and you're free without responsibility.' But I was only free to serve. I never asked about my rights, my comfort, or my life. But now I ask you: Have you ever thought, even once, about what I need?"

Nahla's words opened deep wounds in her mother's heart, wounds that couldn't be healed with silence. Her mother looked at her, tears streaming down her cheeks, and whispered in a trembling voice:

"So you're determined. How will you live alone? Omar is in another town, and being away from home is harsh?"

Nahla answered in a calm but firm voice:

"I'll try my luck, Mom. I have nothing to lose. And if I fail, I know the family's door won't be closed in my face."

A heavy silence fell. The mother's gaze was broken, full of confusion and disappointment.

As for Nahla, she realized that the hour had struck, and that leaving was a necessity, not an option. She entered her room, sat at the desk, and pulled out her old notebook, her outlet. She opened it to a new page and wrote:

"Sometimes, you don't leave everything behind because you're weak, but because you're finally certain that you're strong enough to start over."

She closed the notebook and leaned back in her chair, knowing that tomorrow would not be easy because the next battle would be with her brothers. But for the first time in her life, she wasn't afraid. She was prepared, and she knew what she wanted.

(2)
My Voice That You Have Never Heard Before

The weakness imposed on us throughout our lives... does not mean that we do not have strength, but rather that the days did not allow us to show it.

The next morning, Nahla woke up early, filled with a rare sense of serenity and a strength she hadn't experienced in years. She prepared breakfast for the family, smiling, as if a huge burden had been lifted from her. She entered her mother's room to wake her up, but found her still lying on her bed, pleading her usual tiredness and exhaustion.

Nahla smiled quietly, then kissed her mother's forehead, saying tenderly: "Good morning, Mom. Breakfast is ready."

But she didn't wait for approval. For the first time, she was doing what she felt was right, without fear or hesitation, supported by the shadow of her older brother Omar, who had always been her support and the voice of reason in her life. After breakfast, Nahla sat next to her mother in the kitchen.

The moment was tense, but she smiled, trying to ease the tension. Then, in a pleading voice, she said:

"My dear mother, I'm going to the clinic for the required medical examination. Do you need anything before I leave?"

Her mother gave her a harsh look and replied coldly:

"No, I'll start depending on myself from now on. I don't need your help." Nahla smiled sadly and hugged her despite her reluctance:

"My dear mother... I won't leave you. Just please, for the first time, accept my decision. Don't say I'm not satisfied or I don't agree... Just say, 'I'm with you.' I want to feel like I have the right to make my own decisions, even once in my life. And if this trip doesn't work out, it's just a visit, and I'll be back."

The silence was heavier than any refusal. Her mother didn't speak, but a fearful tear betrayed her confusion. Then she suddenly asked, "Where will you be staying?"

Nahla answered reassuringly:

"Maha is Alaa's friend. She found me a room with a private bathroom with a family near the university in Toronto. My brother Omar is only an hour away; he lives in Mississauga."

But soon, anger spread across her mother's face, and she said sharply:

"You decided everything and planned every detail without any of us knowing. Your brother Ayad will lose his mind when he finds out, and so will the rest of the family."

Nahla fell silent, then said in a voice laced with pain:

"Come on, Mom, which family are you referring to? Did any of them consult you before they left? Or did they tell you when they bought their homes?

They only told you after everything was done, and you accepted it with love. As for me, even today I ask permission to go out with my friends. Isn't that enough? Isn't it time for me to live, too?"

The mother's gaze broke, and for the first time, she looked defeated by her daughter's words. She didn't answer, just cried silently. Then she said in a choked-up voice:

"So... you're determined?"

Nahla hadn't expected to see her mother cry like that. She felt a pang of guilt, but there was an inner voice that wouldn't shut up, saying:

"You've been late enough, and we must hurry."

She walked towards the balcony overlooking the sea, looked at the horizon, at the waves that were crashing as if they were screaming for freedom, and closed her eyes to inhale some determination, and exhale what remained of her fear.

She said to herself:

"I'm not running away... I'm just looking for myself."

She walked back slowly, standing in front of her mother, who tried to stand as if to say, with her exhausted body:

"Can't you see my exhaustion?"

Nahla said in a voice that sounded like a confession:

"Mother... I know you're not satisfied with me. But, since when have you been satisfied with me, satisfied, and agreeing to whatever I intend to do? Look back, you'll find that I've sacrificed a lot, and all I gained was the fear of your anger. I always sought your approval, but you placed more restrictions around me. As for my siblings, I lived with them contentedly, and despite their sudden decisions regarding every job or travel, you never thought of opposing them. Why am I the only one who should be held accountable for every action I take?"

The mother burst into tears again. The tears were hot, tinged with anger and a belated confession, but she didn't respond. Her words were like a deep wound reopened after years of concealment. For the first time, her mother seemed to feel her daughter's pain. Her eyes were filled with sympathy mixed with intense anger that her lips could not express.

But her facial expressions spoke volumes. She even rose with difficulty from her chair, her body swaying left and right, as if to tell Nahla of her weakness and exhaustion, as if to say:

"Don't you see how tired I am of this life?"

In the past, this familiar situation had always forced Nahla to back down and submit to her mother's wishes. But today, she knew deep down that her mother's weakness and exhaustion could completely control her life if she surrendered to them again. She watched her mother in loving silence, allowing her to regain her balance for a few moments before responding in a sad voice, saying:

"Forgive me, Mother, if I hurt your heart. You may not understand me now, but I'm finally beginning to understand myself."

She quietly closed the door behind her... not running away, but departing for a life she had been waiting for, for a long time. Nahla was certain that she would change her life to search for herself. After she left, she muttered to herself:

"The time has come... I am still alive, and this decision is not an escape, but rather a path to search for my lost self."

Chapter Seven

(1)
When Truth Turns into a Scream

In every fateful decision, you will find those who stand in your way not because they hate you, but because they fear your power.

When Nahla left the house, her mother's state was not devoid of anger and tension. At that moment, her mother's phone rang, and the caller on the other end was Omar. As soon as she answered the line, she showered him with words of blame and reproach, without greeting him. She said to him:

"What right do you have to decide concerning Nahla without telling me?" Omar replied to her very calmly:

"Good morning, my beloved mother. I see that you have decided to wage war on my precious beloved. Give me a few moments so that I can explain the matter to you."

His mother responded forcefully:

"What do you want to tell me after this bad news?" Omar calmly replied:

"Mother, Nahla has grown up and has the right to choose her own life. She hasn't left her family; she'll travel to find herself, and I'm close to her, in the same country."

His mother responded angrily, saying:

"How could you allow your sister to live far away from her family in a foreign country? If she were with you, I would have said yes and agreed, but you are far away from her."

Omar heard her words and said:

"My dear mother, I believe that Nahla is the one who makes the decision. She hasn't overstepped her bounds. She just found the opportunity, like any other family member, and wants to try her luck and change her life for the better. I am very convinced, and let everyone know, that I will support her and be by her side until she finds herself again. If she ever wants to return, the decision will be hers as well."

His mother responded harshly:

"I repeat for the thousandth time: you have no right to determine your sister's fate without my knowledge and consent."

Omar's response was somewhat harsh, as he said:

"My dear mother, I want to tell you something. Nahla has suffered greatly, and for the first time, I've seen the youngest sibling not get their due share of life. She has surrendered many things and entrusted herself to you and the rest of the siblings. Each person was controlling her as they wished. It was like a game of ping-pong, always going according to the opinion of whoever felt responsible for her. I don't know who gave them guardianship to control her life. She hasn't had a chance in life... I also confirm that I have been very negligent in my duties to her, and I hope to make up for some of the neglect and lack of consideration. That's why I have decided to stand by her until she makes her way through life as she sees fit. And there is something very important. Tell me, for God's sake, don't I have the right, as a brother, to have my sister live with me and for me to look after her?

Nahla has sought refuge from me, and I don't want to disappoint her. This matter is not beyond your control; it is her right, and she must get her due share of life. I will contact Ayad and Adhraa and inform them of the matter."

His mother couldn't answer him and ended the call angrily.

More than two days have passed. Nahla avoided talking to her mother about the trip. She was still angry and couldn't comprehend that Nahla would leave her and travel to a distant country. She tried to appease her mother while she was having coffee with her at a café in a shopping mall. In a calm voice, she said:

"Are you still mad at me, Mom?" Her mother responded angrily:

"Nahla, can you imagine? You'll travel to a continent far away from me, different in every way, and most importantly, I won't see you."

Nahla responded calmly:

"Mom, it's only two years of school, and I'll visit you during the summer vacation. My brother Omar promised to visit me whenever he has the chance, especially on weekends. At the same time, I'll look for a job, and even if I don't find one, the amount I've saved is enough for living expenses, transportation, and rent. Mom, I need this trip to rebuild my life and think about my future. It's a golden opportunity for me, and I hope you pray for my success."

Her mother's tears flowed uncontrollably, and she said, her voice breaking with sobs:

"I can't live a single day without you, Nahla. How will I bear your absence for two years?

Nahla was hurt by her mother's words and hugged her tightly, trying to ease her tension. At the same time, she tried to remain composed and said to her:

"Mom, it's only been two years, and you're not alone. Ayad and Adhraa are with you, and Jumana will come after her daughter's wedding to stay with you for two months. Nadine has also decided to stay with you for several months. You won't miss me much; you have enough loved ones to occupy your time."

Her mother suddenly interrupted her, as if revealing a long-kept secret:

"Is that why you're leaving me? Because of Jumana and Nadine. I admit that I've wronged you, especially when I rejected the suitor who recently proposed to you, but is this my punishment? That you'll leave me and go far away from me? Is it because you're angry with me that you're punishing me by traveling and abandoning me?"

Nahla took a deep breath and tried to hold back the tears that had begun to well up in her eyes. Then she said:

"Mom, you even rejected my martyred fiancé, Nidal. If it weren't for my insistence, and after four years of attempts and pleading, you wouldn't have agreed. Even after my engagement, you claimed that the marriage wouldn't happen because you weren't convinced of it. The engagement lasted for three years, during which I endured all the pain and bullying from my family. I don't know the real reason why you rejected Nidal as my husband, especially from my brothers, whom you always supported against me, especially Jumana.

Ultimately, my marriage did not happen... He was martyred on the battlefield. For God's sake, tell me, why did you refuse my marriage and bless the marriages of my brothers and sisters?"

Nahla continued, her voice tinged with bitterness:

As for the last groom, when she saw that I was determined to marry him, you spoke to him behind my back and without my knowledge, saying, 'I will die if you marry Nahla and she leaves me." He apologized and went home. He was impeccable—a widower, a university professor, with grown, married children, and his age was suitable for me. This was my last chance... Do you know, Mother, what Adhra said when I told her about your rejection of him? She said, "My mother has the right to refuse. Tell me, you are the one who will take care of my mother, as I go to work every day, and sometimes my work requires me to travel for several days. Ayad lives in another emirate, and the rest of the brothers and sisters live far from us. Is this the real reason for your rejection, Mother?"

A heavy silence fell between mother and daughter, as if time stood still for a moment. Nahla looked into her mother's eyes, seeking an answer she had always searched for, but today she was searching for something deeper. With regret and tears in her eyes, Nahla continued:

"Mother, for God's sake, don't you realize that I'm fifty years old, and this groom was my last chance to own a home and live my life independently. Why do you oppose every step I take? Even worse, why do you allow Jumana and Adhraa to control your decisions regarding me? Why do you let their voices rise above mine, as if I'm incompetent, especially Jumana, who always incites you against me?"

The mother's feelings were mixed with pain and anger, and she said in a faltering voice:

"My daughter, all I wanted was to ensure your well-being. You're the youngest of your brothers and sisters, and out of my concern for you and my fear that time would betray you... I didn't know what to do or how to protect you, so I turned to your sisters for advice."

Nahla looked at her with tearful eyes and replied:

"Mother, you still haven't answered my question. Why does Jumana always interfere in our lives, even when she's outside the home? Please, don't oppose my decision this time. I earned the money through my hard work, from my sewing work, and from the center where I work. For your information, as I told you, I have submitted my resignation from the center, and this decision is irrevocable. Please comfort me, support me, agree, and wish me success."

Her mother was silent for a moment, then said in a broken voice: "Nahla, are you punishing me because I refused the groom?" Nahla smiled sadly and said:

"No, Mother. I did not mean that. Marriage is fate, but I want to feel, even once, that I am free to make my own decisions, that I have the right to think... and choose my future."

Her mother closed her eyes, as if trying to absorb her daughter's words. But Nahla knew that the decision to leave had become inevitable, and that she needed this opportunity no matter the cost. She was fully convinced that freedom does not wait, but rather is courageously seized by hearts that refuse to break.

(2)
When Departure is Salvation

Not all cruelty is escape. Sometimes absence is a rescue for what remains of us. True pain is not born from departure, but from the silence of the years you lived among us without a voice.

The days passed quickly, and Nahla didn't feel that time was beginning to fold its hours, as if it were speeding her towards a new station on the train of life. She sat alone in her room that night, staring at the ceiling with a lost gaze, as if searching for an answer or perhaps the courage to face tomorrow. She laid her head on the pillow and took a deep breath to expel her creeping fear. She began to think about the future, university, the new life, and the responsibilities she would bear away from everyone.

She turned her eyes towards her small desk near the window, where her laptop was open on the flight booking page, while she remained stuck between her dreams and her fear of the next step. Her phone suddenly rang, the tone breaking the silence that filled the room.

She looked at the screen and saw Omar's name. He was coming full of enthusiasm.

He said:

"Nahla, we won, my sweetheart. Things are going as we planned. There's only a little left. I can't describe my happiness. I'm counting the days and hours until I see you."

Nahla shed light tears that mixed with a satisfied smile. She held the phone tightly, as if grasping the feeling of security she had been searching for for a while, and said in a low voice:

"Omar… I still can't believe that I was accepted into university. I can't believe that I would leave everything and start over. But, honestly, I'm scared… scared to face our brothers. I'm afraid that they will disappoint me."

Omar replied, his voice loud and full of confidence, as if removing the anxiety from her heart:

"Nahla, we've overcome the most difficult part, and all that's left is to put the final step in place. Don't worry, I'll take care of everything. I'll talk to

Adhra and Ayad, and tell them that I have the right to have my sister with me and support me. Let me face everyone this time."

Nahla felt a sudden sense of relief, as if Omar's words had reorganized her thoughts. But he didn't stop there and continued, laughing to ease the tension:

"When you arrive safely, I will stay with you for a whole week. I will accompany you to complete your paperwork at the university, and I will ensure that your accommodation is comfortable. However, I don't understand why you refuse to stay with us at my house? The distance between us is only an hour!"

Nahla laughed for the first time in days and said lightly:

"Let me breathe independence, Omar. I want to live on my own, even if only for a little while. And if I go bankrupt, I will accept your offer and stay with you."

He shared her laughter and said tenderly:

"As you wish, my little one, but always remember that I am near you and have never left you. Walk with confidence, and God's eye is watching over you."

She ended the call feeling as if her heart had become lighter. She put the phone aside and relaxed on the bed. She looked at the ceiling again, but this time with different eyes. She felt that tomorrow was not as frightening as it had seemed to her before, but rather an opportunity. Then her thoughts returned to her mother, to that farewell that awaited her. She thought about her tears and the difficulty of leaving her behind, but she realized that this step was necessary and that the pain is temporary. She whispered to herself:

"Of course I'll miss them, and maybe they'll be angry, but this path is mine alone. I need to live my dream. I need to live for Nahla."

She finally closed her eyes, feeling as if she had stepped onto the first rung of a new ladder. It wasn't easy, but she knew that the journey to freedom began with a brave step, and that her independence wouldn't be given to her... she had to take it with the courage of her heart.

The next morning, Nahla woke up to the sound of her mother preparing breakfast in the kitchen. She felt a mixture of sadness as her mother set the table. She knew her mother loved her deeply and didn't want her to be apart from her even for a single day, but this step was necessary for her to prove that she could make her own decisions. She entered the kitchen and sat silently next to her mother. The words between them were few, but their looks held a deep meaning. Nahla reached out, gently took her mother's hand, and kissed it. She said in a calm voice:

"Mom, I know you're worried about me and want to protect me, but I need to live my own life. I'll always be the person you know, and I'll return to you as soon as I can. If you need me, trust me, I'll be there for you as soon as possible."

Her mother looked at her, smiled a small smile full of tenderness and pain at the same time, and said:

"I am with you, Nahla. I will pray to God to grant you success and protect you in every step you take."

Nahla was surprised by her mother's words. They made her feel relieved, as if a huge weight had been lifted from her shoulders. Her mother's approval was very important, and she had now achieved a great accomplishment with her mother's approval for the travel.

Chapter Eight

(1)
Facing the Family

True strength lies not in your ability to overcome others, but in your ability to overcome yourself and transcend your fears.

The hours of the day passed slowly and heavily for Nahla, as gloom was evident on the faces of all family members. For the first time, Adhraa was unable to impose her control and decisions on Nahla's fate. The reason was both simple and important: Adhraa hadn't given Nahla the money.

Rather, she and the entire family were surprised, especially when they learned that Nahla had obtained a visa to study in Canada. Even Ayad, her brother, who was known for his strict rejection of everything, found himself faced with an unchangeable fait accompli. He realized that any objection or problem that might be caused would simply make Nahla to pack her bags and leave the house before the travel time, so everyone preferred to remain silent.

At lunchtime, when the family gathered around the table, the spacious dining room offered a panoramic view of the Abu Dhabi Corniche. The sea glittered in the silver sunlight, and on the horizon, ships and boats could be seen. The large glass window overlooking the sea painted a charming panoramic picture, adding a distinctive beauty to the Corniche, blending with the splendor of the dining room.

Despite the enchanting view and the tranquility inside the house, the atmosphere was somewhat tense. The rectangular, dark-wood table was laden with a variety of Iraqi-style dishes, but no one seemed interested in the taste of the food or the beauty of the scenery outside. Everyone inside was wondering about Nahla's plans, while the lunch table gathered them, where tension lingered for a few minutes. The main topic of the family, which dominated the atmosphere, was inquiring about Nahla's meal. Every family member wanted to chime in, but they couldn't until Adhra broke the silence and asked Nahla:

"Why didn't you tell me about your travel plans, how you've arranged your affairs, and where you'll be staying?"

Nahla answered calmly and confidently:

"I told my mother, and I'll repeat it now. Maha, Alaa's friend, rented me a room with a bathroom at her friend's and neighbor's place. I paid the rent for three months in advance, and she lives in Toronto, near the university.

As for the money, as you know, I work at the sewing center and have saved a lot of money from my work there. I also sold my gold, in addition to the money I received at the end of my service at the center. My brother Omar surprised me by paying my first year's tuition and told me it was his gift.

God willing, I'll have enough money to find a job there."

The faint sound of waves in the distance filled the tense atmosphere inside the room, but no one paid attention. Ayad broke the silence with a

skeptical tone:

"And if you fail, what will you do if you run out of money?"

Nahla looked at him from the corner of her eye for a moment, speaking confidently for the first time. She said:

"My residency in the UAE is valid for six months, and the center manager told me she wouldn't cancel it if I returned during this period." If I don't succeed in my studies or find a job opportunity, I will return as well.

Omar also said that he is with me and that he and his family will meet me. At the airport, Ayad, I am not going to an unknown place. In any case, do not worry. I will do my best not to fail."

Adhraa suddenly laughed sarcastically and said:

"Do you think you'll succeed in sewing? Working in the West isn't like working here. Their tastes are different, and they don't look for someone who doesn't have a degree or extensive experience. You're not a skilled designer. Do you think you can compete with top designers?"

Nahla was hurt by Adhraa's ridicule and well-known bullying, but she controlled her emotions and said calmly:

"I'm not thinking about design, but rather working in sewing and embroidery. Then I'll go study a speciality I have experience in and require an international certificate: healthcare and life sciences. Just like you did when you traveled to Europe and Malaysia to bolster your career with specialized certificates. I thought the same way; you're my role model."

Adhraa responded in her usual stern tone:

"Why all this travel and suffering? Wouldn't it be better to find yourself here in your job? Would you abandon your family to explore yourself? What a pointless philosophy."

Nahla responded confidently and calmly after looking at her sideways for a few moments and said:

"Excuse me, sister. Didn't you travel to Europe to obtain a one-year certificate of experience in the stock market and securities? Didn't you travel to Malaysia for a year for the same purpose? Didn't you say you wanted to develop yourself?"

Adhraa was silent for a moment, then said sharply:

"Of course, and that was for work and to earn a good income so I could help you."

Nahla smiled calmly and said:

"Yes, but that was for you first, and I don't deny your kindness. I'll never forget how you told me to quit my job and take care of my mother, even though you didn't even remind me that caring for my mother is my duty. Caring for my mother and ensuring her comfort is a duty for all children.

May God protect her for all of us. You also suggested giving me money. My question now is: If you had the opportunity to travel to Canada to study, would you cancel it for the sake of the family, or would you say to yourself, 'I deserve a little rest."

A heavy silence fell over the room; even the waves outside seemed to have stopped. Adhraa became furious, but she couldn't find the right words to respond. A spark of pent-up anger appeared in her eyes. She clenched her fists and held herself together. For the first time, she couldn't yell at Nahla or blame her for anything.

They continued eating in silence, but they no longer tasted anything. The food had completely lost its flavor. Their feelings also cooled, and the warmth of the moment between the family members faded.

(2)
The Calm Before the Storm

And in the moment of silence between two words, a flower grows in the heart, watered by dreams and made to grow by wishes.

The days passed quickly, as if time was saying to Nahla, "Hurry, time is gold." Several weeks later, one unusually quiet evening in the family home, the great hall, which had always been filled with the sound of the usual conversations, was drowned in heavy silence.

The place seemed charged with pent-up emotions that had not been announced. It was the evening before the promised departure, and it was as if everyone preferred to be lost in their own thoughts.

Ayad, with his sharp features, who was in his mid-fifties, sat on the couch reading the newspaper.

His eyes would move between the lines, but he wasn't really concentrating on what he was reading. Ayad's medium build and his neat black hair made him a strong, silent presence, but he preferred not to get involved in any conversation about Nahla's travel. He always used to impose his opinion, and whoever confronted him had to obey, not argue. With his mother's acceptance, he turned the newspaper over several times in an attempt to ease the heavy silence surrounding the place.

As for Adhraa, the older sister, she was in her early sixties, a dignified woman with a distinctive presence, a domineering personality and a narcissistic streak. Her personality was filled with love and concern for family as she saw fit. Her hair was gray, scattered among brown strands. She loved the word "I". She sat at a small desk by the window, working on her laptop, as if trying to escape the tense atmosphere of work. She was always the type to impose her opinion on others, and she rarely went back on her decisions. Her mature features and distinctive beauty gave her an air of majesty, but her gaze was preoccupied with something other than work.

As for the mother, time had tarnished her features, but she maintained her eyes filled with emotion. She sat silently watching the television. She thought she was following the news, but her mind was elsewhere, and from time to time she would steal glances at Nahla, as if trying to understand what was going on in her daughter's mind.

Nahla sat in her rocking chair, sipping her coffee slowly, trying to calm her turbulent thoughts. At that moment, she looked like a strong woman. Her face was lined with wrinkles, shadowed by her chestnut hair, reflecting the turmoil in her chest.

Everyone was drowning in a frantic calm, waiting for the looming storm. Despite the conflicting emotions, the premonition of separation was looming over the evening. Nahla felt the pressure of the silence almost suffocating her, so she decided to break it. She raised her head calmly and looked at her mother, who was watching television. She said in a voice audible to everyone:

"Mother... I've booked the flight tickets. It will be from Dubai in a week, God willing, and I'll be staying at Alaa's house in Sharjah for three days before my departure."

Her mother raised her eyes from the television and looked at Nahla with a sad expression. She spoke these words, but in a broken voice:

"To this extent, do you want to rush our separation?" Or because you knew Jumana would be coming in two weeks to stay with us for two months? She brought forward her departure date to say goodbye.

Nahla felt her mother's words weighing heavily on her, and despite trying to maintain her composure, she responded in a voice full of reproach.

"Mother, why did you tell Jumana? Is it because you're certain of her alleged love for me, or because you can't hide anything from her?"

Nahla was silent for a few moments, as if gathering her strength, then continued in a low, bitter tone:

"Please, Mother, don't open the old books"... even though her wounds were still bleeding.

The mother listened to her words before leaving, sensing that the conversation had taken a painful turn. However, Nahla didn't stop, as if the words were flowing from her without barriers. Before Nahla could respond to her mother, Ayad left the house, while Adhra left the living room and went to her room, making it clear with her actions that she didn't want to hear any unwanted additions and didn't want to argue or quarrel with Nahla. Nahla waited a few moments and said:

"Remember, Mother, when I took out a loan from the bank? I was full of ambition, and I told you I was going to buy an apartment in Erbil to secure my future. But you begged me to give the money to Jumana and her husband? Because they are going through financial hardship. I gave you the money to give to her, Mom, but you didn't tell her it was from me. You told her that you provided it with your own money.?

She paused for a moment, her mind going back to that bitter moment:

"I spent years paying the bank installments, while Jumana bought a car for her son with the money. When I asked her, she coldly said, "You have no right to ask me. I took the money from my mother."

The mother listened silently, her eyes brimming with tears, but she couldn't respond. She felt she had made a mistake and that she had indirectly caused this deep wound. Nahla continued, but in a calmer voice:

"Mother, you're the one who made Jumana look like my enemy. You took advantage of your excessive love for her, and I became… You even treat her children like your favorite grandchildren, while I was always in the shadows."

The mother sighed deeply, as if carrying a mountain of regret in her heart. But Nahla, despite the bitterness of the conversation, wanted to end it gently:

"Mother, please let me go in peace. I will visit you whenever I have the chance, and we will talk daily via WhatsApp. I want to leave with your prayers, not with blame."

After the heavy conversation between mother and daughter ended, she stood up. Nahla gently told her mother that she was going out to buy some travel supplies, would meet up with her friends and colleagues to say goodbye, and would not be back for dinner.

Nahla left the house feeling a mixture of relief and sadness. She headed to the market to buy what she needed, then met her friends at the Al-Maskouf Al-Iraqi Restaurant on Airport Street.

The meeting was full of laughter and beautiful memories, as if time had stopped for a moment to give her a chance to enjoy the company of her loved ones.

After dinner, she went with her friends to the beach. They sat on the sand in front of the sea, sipping "Karak" tea, their laughter filling the place. The atmosphere was full of contradictory feelings: comfort, nostalgia, and fear of the unknown.

Chapter Nine

(1)
Whisper of Departure

The fear of departure does not frighten those who carry a dream and hope in their hearts, but rather becomes a step toward the self.

Nahla returned home that evening, mentally preparing to leave.

Despite the pain of separation, she knew that her journey was a new beginning, and that she would need strength and determination to face what awaited her. She sat alone in her room, contemplating the unknown ahead. She felt afraid, but there was hope within her for a better future. In a moment, as if she wanted to escape reality, she went to her most beautiful memories. As if she wanted to gather her strength, to have a strong motivation for change, she closed her eyes and immersed herself in the most beautiful days of her life. There are small moments hidden in memory, but they light up life whenever the road gets dark.

She remembered that rainy day in December, a month after her relationship with Nidal began. Her friends, Howayda and Alaa, were heading to school under heavy clouds. They hadn't brought umbrellas; they had left the house in a hurry, and she hadn't expected the rain to fall so heavily. It began to rain heavily, and the wind made the air even colder, but they continued walking, trying to shield themselves from the cold raindrops with their hands. They laughed together despite the wetness, while the rain dripped onto their faces and made their hair stick to their foreheads.

Then, amidst the fog and rain, Nidal suddenly appeared. He was standing by the side of the road, holding a large black umbrella, protecting himself from the rain even though he was driving. However, he got out of his car and walked a distance until he reached them.

When Nahla saw him, she was astonished. She couldn't believe Nidal was here; this wasn't his place. She knew he was at the battlefront, so how could he be here now? But before she could think further, he walked towards them with a warm smile and addressed Nahla:

"Nahla, be careful. The road is muddy, and the heavy rain might make you sick."

She couldn't hide her surprise at his sudden appearance, but he quickly pulled her out of her confusion. He quickly handed her the umbrella, covered her head and the heads of her friends, and said:

"Take this umbrella. I don't want you to get sick from the rain."

He said it in a gentle tone and with a slight smile, then cast a friendly glance at Howayda and Alaa and nodded to them in greeting. Nahla felt a heat surge across her cheeks, not just from shyness, but from Nidal's kindness and concern.

She had never expected that there would be someone to care for her in this way, especially in a simple situation like this. She said in a slightly trembling voice, trying to hide her confusion:

"Thank you, Nidal. I didn't expect you to be here. Aren't you supposed to be at the battlefront?"

Nidal replied with a calm smile:

"I came on an errand and was passing by and saw you. I can't leave you out in the rain without an umbrella."

Howayda and Alaa stood surprised, but bright smiles quickly spread across their faces. Howayda said cheerfully:

"Oh, Nidal, you're today's hero."

Everyone laughed, and Nahla felt a strange warmth creep into her heart, as if the cold raindrops no longer affected her.

At that moment, she realized that Nidal wasn't just a passing person in her life, but someone who genuinely cared for her and was ready to be by her side even in the simplest moments. She took the umbrella and thanked him again.

At that moment, she felt her heart filled with new feelings for him. This rainy day was the beginning of a new story, a love story that began under the rain, with an umbrella and a simple gesture that meant a lot.

(2)
Broken Dream

Not all endings come by choice; sometimes they are imposed upon us by those who fail to understand our hearts.

Nahla was once again immersed in her memories of the past, recalling the day that had turned her life upside down.

The days went by, and the months brought their beautiful moments and her wonderful platonic relationship with Nidal. But one day, unexpectedly, while she was walking with Nidal on one of the streets of Adhamiya, her older sister Jumana, who was eight years older, saw them and quickly told her mother what she had seen.

Her mother's reaction wasn't easy. She scolded her severely, and for the first time in her life, her mother hit and slapped her hard. Jumana was the great instigator.

She wasn't the older sister who would kindly advise her younger sister if she made a mistake. Instead, she saw a great opportunity to get Nahla and, at the same time, win her mother's approval. Nahla's mother asked for

Nidal's address, then went to his house and told him to end their relationship. She also threatened to tell her father and brothers if she didn't break up with him immediately. Nahla felt intense pain and had no choice but to obey her mother's commands.

A week later, Nahla received a message from Nidal through her friend Howayda, who lived next door to his house. He reassured her that he was still faithful and that he was waiting for her to graduate from high school so he could propose. Her heart filled with joy and hope. Nidal would occasionally send her messages and photos he'd taken of her on her way to and from school, all containing reassuring words and a promise that he would be with her no matter what. Nahla kept those messages and photos with her friend Howayda, fearing that her mother or sister would find them.

She closed her memories and ended the night with prayer and supplication. Afterwards, she fell asleep and slept peacefully. Between the sadness of parting and the hope for change, her heart whispered to her:

"Tomorrow will give you a new beginning."

Chapter Ten

(1)
Farewell

Parting is the pain that sharpens our souls, but hope is the bridge that guides us to a new reunion.

On the morning of July 7, 2015, the farewell was more heartbreaking than Nahla had expected. After gathering her strength, she stood before her mother, her sister Adhraa, and her brother Ayad. She sensed that her tears, despite her efforts to hide them, had betrayed her and revealed her feelings. She struggled to keep herself composed in front of them, but she knew that moment would be forever etched in her memory. She called a taxi to take her to Sharjah, where her friend Alaa lived. Every step toward the car felt like it was bringing her closer to the hardest goodbye.

When the moment finally arrived, she hugged her mother tightly, as if searching for all the comfort she could get. In a trembling voice, her words thick with tears, she whispered:

My beloved mother... my heaven and my life, please pray for me... pray that God grants me success, for your prayers will not be rejected."

Her mother tried to hold herself together, but she couldn't. Mothers' hearts cannot bear to be separated from their daughters. As she wiped away her tears with a trembling hand, she replied:

"I pray to God to grant you safety in every step you take, and that you return to me safely, my light."

Nahla looked at her mother with a pained smile, laden with a thousand emotions, and then said:

"If I fail, I will return. I have a valid six-month residency in the UAE. If I succeed, I will work hard to invite you to live with me."

Her sister, Adhraa, who was standing there, unable to believe what was happening, approached her. She hugged her tightly and said in a broken voice:

"If I have ever wronged or hurt you, please forgive me."

Nahla responded with a voice filled with compassion, her tears no longer able to be held back as they fell:

"You, in particular, my beloved sister. I have nothing but goodness for you. You have always been a father and a mother to me in particular, and to all of us. At a time when we needed someone to stand by us, whether during the harsh days of the siege in Baghdad or here in Abu Dhabi, on the contrary, I am the one asking you to forgive me."

Afterwards, she turned to Ayad, who, as usual, stood silent at such moments. He was unable to express his feelings in words. But Nahla felt everything he was unable to express, and she responded with words filled with love and gratitude after hugging him tightly:

"My beloved brother Ayad, I ask God to protect you and grant you success in your life."

Ayad couldn't respond, so he simply hugged her tightly. His tears, which he had long held back, began to fall silently. He walked her to the car in silence, heavy with pain. When she reached the door, before she got in, he asked her in a broken voice, overflowing with grief:

"Why did you refuse to let me drive you?" She looked at him with tearful eyes and said:

"Because I want this moment of farewell to remain etched in my memory.

I don't want us to repeat the farewells. We've turned a page in our lives, and now we're starting a new one."

Her words were like an arrow that pierced Ayad's heart, touching the deepest feelings of separation and heartache, and they remain etched in his memory to this day. She got into the car and drove off, leaving behind a farewell that will remain etched in everyone's hearts, intertwined with fifty years of love, challenges, and hope for a new future.

Nahla sat in the back seat of the car, feeling the soft leather seat beneath her as the car gently rocked and rolled toward Sharjah. The road from Abu Dhabi passed through Dubai, and with every curve or bump, the monotonous sound of the engine and the soft music in the background blended with the sounds of cars speeding on both sides of the road.

Through the window, she watched the modern buildings rise along the road, contemplating the clear sky and the rays of the early morning sun, casting a warm hue over everything. She felt a light breeze drift through the window, gently caressing her skin as if caressing her memories.

As she contemplated the road, she remembered when she came with her family in the 1990s. The road to Sharjah passed through vast sand dunes, the sun reflecting off the sand, filling the space with the magic of the picturesque desert.

Today, that desert has turned into a jungle of high-rise buildings and modern bridges, making her feel that time has passed faster than she expected. She muttered to herself, her voice barely audible over the music: "More than twenty years have passed... How did it go by so quickly?"

She recalled the years of laughter, exhaustion, and the scent of incense that filled the exhibitions and bazaars where she displayed her designs, as well as the voices of customers discussing her abayas and children's fashions. Every small success was a spark of joy that filled her heart, and the buzz of the exhibitions filled her with a sense of contentment.

But what moved her feelings even more deeply were the memories of her work at the Center for People with Special Needs. She remembered the sounds of children laughing, the smell of the morning coffee she drank with her colleagues, the sounds of the hallways, and the touch of small hands clasping hers for help.

"Oh God..." she said in a trembling voice as she recalled the moment her work at the center ended. At that moment, she felt a deep emptiness in her chest, especially during her final days, when the children presented her with an orange Kashmiri shawl, embroidered with the colors of beautiful wildflowers, as a gift. That was one of the most difficult days for her.

At that moment, the ringing of the phone interrupted her thoughts as if to awaken her from her reverie. It was Alaa's lively voice on the other end, carrying with it the warmth of an old friendship that had not changed.

Nahla closed her eyes for a moment and listened to Alaa's voice as she smiled. She felt as if a part of her heart still found a safe haven among her old friends, despite everything that had changed around her.

"Nahla, where have you gotten to?"

Nahla looked at the road and said with a smile:

"I'm at the end of Sheikh Zayed Road. If we skip this traffic, I'll be there in half an hour."

Alaa laughed enthusiastically:

"Great! I have a surprise for you."

Nahla smiled back and asked curiously:

"I wonder what it is? I want to know now." Alaa replied, laughing:

"No, no, no... You have to wait. In addition, I've prepared a schedule for the next two days that will be full of surprises and outings, so we can create memories that will last a lifetime when you live in Canada."

Nahla felt gratitude flooding her heart, and she said gently: You're so amazing, Alaa! But what about your work?

Alaa replied enthusiastically:

I took a week off, especially to spend this time with you.

After the call ended, Nahla leaned back in her seat, lost in thought once again, and whispered to herself:

"Indeed, life, as I see it now, does not always give second chances, but today I am living a moment that I will carry with me forever."

(2)
The Wonderful Surprise

Friends are the bridges that take us back to our past, no matter how crowded the present is

About half an hour after Alaa's call, Nahla arrived at her loyal friend's home in Sharjah. That house wasn't just a home; it was a warm haven and a safe haven that carried her to Baghdad. Every time she entered, every corner whispered memory of her homeland: the distinctive scent of perfume, the fragrant Iraqi food that wafted from the kitchen, and even the décor, which was heavily influenced by Baghdad, from paintings that spoke of Baghdad's alleys to sofas decorated with turquoise and blue patterns mixed with yellow... the colors of Iraq.

She loved sitting in a room Alaa called "the Baghdad sitting room," where Iraqi rugs covered the floor and a simple diwan hosted gatherings. In a cozy corner, Alaa placed the "mangala," copper coffee pots, and coffee cups decorated with motifs representing Iraqi civilization from north to south. Even the atmosphere of the room resembled Baghdad. When Nahla rang the doorbell, Howaida, her friend who had arrived from Riyadh that morning, opened the door. Howaida, the absent yet present, was embraced by Nahla with intense longing, a mixture of laughter and tears, as if time had taken them back to their first meeting.

Five minutes of hugs and words intertwined with emotions passed in the blink of an eye before Alaa invited them to sit in the "diwan" room. They sat as if they had once been children again, each eager to hear from the other, and memories began to flow without permission. Nahla took the initiative, congratulating Howayda:

"My dear Howayda, congratulations on your son Ahmed's graduation, and thank God for the wonderful job at Saudi Airlines, and congratulations on entering university... All that's left is for you to marry Ahmed off, and then we'll see you as a grandmother. You've grown up, Howayda!"

Howayda laughed a pure laugh and said jokingly:

"No, Nahla, I'm like you. I stopped counting at 21. I don't want to grow up."

Alaa interrupted them with a smile:

"Me too, I'm still 21... just like you."

They laughed for a long time, and Nahla said with a gentle chuckle:

"That's unfair. You've married and become grandmothers, and I haven't yet. You're 25, but I'm only 21."

A moment of silence fell before Howayda recalled an unforgettable moment in Nahla's life:

"Do you remember, Nahla, when you forgot your 21st birthday? I called you and told you to meet me at the café where we were staying. When you arrived, a surprise awaited you... Nidal, may God have mercy on him, had brought your birthday cake; it was his idea. He said to you, laughing, "In my eyes, you'll always be that 18-year-old girl."

Silence reigned... That memory struck a sad chord in Nahla's heart, but Alaa was quick to break the silence with a warm smile as she handed Nahla a small box. Inside was a gold chain with a map of Iraq hanging from it, and the names Alaa and Howayda were engraved on the back.

Alaa said gently:

"We wanted to be with you in your exile... This is a token of our love."

Nahla's eyes filled with tears of emotion, and she, in turn, took out another small box and handed it to them. It contained two simple gold rings.

Nahla said in a trembling voice:

"I went to the gold market yesterday and chose these two rings for you. I wanted to leave something of myself with you."

A silence filled with nostalgia and joy, then Alaa spoke, reviving an old memory:

Remember, Nahla, when we said goodbye to you in the old café in Baghdad? I was sure we would meet again in the Emirates. I never felt it was a real goodbye."

Nahla replied, her voice choking:

"Yes... Our meetings continued for years, and our contact never stopped. But this time is different... I will be away from you for years."

Howayda interrupted her, overcome with emotion:

"Nahla, there is no room for separation between us... The connection never ceases, and we never part ways, no matter how far apart we are. Don't count the years; look at how much time has passed without us noticing."

Alaa laughed and said:

"If we keep talking, lunch will get cold and we won't enjoy its taste."

They laughed and went to eat. There, memories of the past sat with them at the table, decorating the table with a special flavor.

After they finished lunch, they returned to the "Diwan" room, a room that had transformed into a haven of memories and dreams. Nostalgia reclined on the ornate sofas, sipping its coffee quietly. As coffee cups swirled between hands, Alaa said in a light, lively tone:

"How about we rest a little, then head out to Al Qasba Canal, then Khalid Lagoon, and then finish off at a lovely, popular café! But no long evenings... tomorrow morning we'll travel to Al Ain."

Howaida raised her eyebrows in surprise and laughed: "The three of us to Al Ain? And why didn't you tell me!" Alaa replied with a confident smile:

"Of course it's a surprise. I've arranged everything... Nahla will meet her friends there. I agreed with them that we will meet at the Mubazzarah, near the mountain "Hafeet". We will spend a beautiful day there and return in the afternoon."

A look of surprise filled Nahla's face, and she asked with amazement mixed with joy:

"Tell me now, sweetheart... which of my friends will I see?"

Alaa replied with a smile, as if she were holding a big secret that she was barely concealing:

"Maryam called me and said that she had arranged the meeting with the rest of my friends, both men and women, and asked me not to tell you, so that it would be a surprise. But you know, I'm not good at keeping secrets."

Nahla burst into laughter, a heartfelt laugh that filled the room with rare warmth, and her eyes lit up with a glimmer of reassurance. At that moment, she wasn't just a woman saying goodbye to her friends, but a soul embracing a lifetime of memories. She felt that those few moments were enough to ease the years of estrangement to come. She was surrounded by her lifelong friends, with stories that never faded, with a love that knew no distance or time could change.

In that simple diwan, all the past and ancient memories were gathered, and the present was revealed in their laughter, a gift engraved on the map of the homeland. As for the future, it stood behind the door, waiting to be knocked on with a smile, promising the most beautiful life.

That night, there was no farewell, but a promise of future meetings, even if the absence was long.

Souls that are truly connected know that distance is just an illusion, and that a meeting is not measured by time, but by longing and intention. And between the warmth of coffee and the whispers of her friends, Nahla realized that even if her heart left, it would never leave....

Chapter Eleven

(1)
The First Moment of Parting

Memories are our passport to the past, but they are also our ticket to creating a future full of moments worth telling.

The next morning, the girls woke up early. Alaa prepared a delicious breakfast that smelled of freshly baked goods. They sat around the table eating "qaymar" and Iraqi "kahi" with cups of hot tea. Conversations and laughter were scattered among them, as if they were anticipating the moments of a beautiful day.

After breakfast, the fun trio set off towards Al Ain, where their friends were waiting for Nahla. They arrived at the mountain "Hafeet", where the nature captivates the heart and the warm sulfurous waters call to the weary souls to relieve their tired bodies of all pain and worry.

The women's pool was like a small oasis of happiness, filled with joy as they swam and exchanged warm splashes. Their laughter filled the space, as if they had been transported back to their teenage years.

As afternoon drew near, everyone gathered for a heartfelt luncheon prepared by Maryam and her lifelong friends for Nahla. Conversations flowed freely, and memories were reignited with each laugh and expression. It was a farewell filled with love and gratitude. At sunset, Nahla stood among them, looked at the faces of her loved ones, and said lovingly:

"Thank you all... You have no idea how close you are to my soul."

Trying to hide her tears, she hugged them one by one, shook hands with her friends, and bid them farewell with love. The fun-loving trio then set off back to Sharjah, carrying with them unforgettable moments. That evening, the trio talked and reminisced about the most beautiful days of their lives: when they were in high school. While they were eating ice cream, Howayda asked Nahla:

"Nahla, do you remember the day we left school and went to eat ice cream on a freezing winter's day at that old café?"

Howayda's question took Nahla back to a very special day in her life, and she said to her:

How beautiful that day was! My first meeting with Nidal took place on December 10, 1982. It was raining, but we weren't cold, and you, Alaa, and I were sitting in that small café in Adhamiya, laughing and eating ice cream. How naive we were. That day, we left school early because the teacher was not there, and we decided to spend some time in the cafeteria. Do you remember, Howayda, the moment we entered the café, and how Nidal was sitting with his friends, sipping tea? I didn't notice his gaze until I went up to pay for the ice cream. At that moment, I was surprised when he stood right in front of me and said with a wide smile, "Isn't it wrong to follow me?" I stood there in amazement, not knowing how to respond. My eyes spoke louder than my tongue, and after a few moments of silence, he added cheerfully, "I'll forgive you if you take my phone number. But on one condition: Don't call me again for a week, because I'll be finishing my military leave."

Nahla continued, with obvious regret:

He gave me his number with a confident smile and then left. Despite my surprise, I took the number from him and never intended to call him again. But Nidal didn't leave things to chance; he followed me until he figured out where I lived.

Her reminiscences were interrupted by Alaa, who said:

"We were all surprised by Nidal's behavior, but it was very bold." Nahla continued:

"The next morning, as I was heading to school, I felt him behind me. He approached me and said, 'Good morning. I would have hated my day if I hadn't greeted you.'" My face flushed with embarrassment, and I stammered as I returned the greeting in a low voice. He added with a smile, "I hope to see you at the café after school. I'll wait for you there." At that moment, I felt a strange connection between me and him, something greater than mere shyness or admiration. I didn't tell you at the time, even though you could have noticed the change in my expression. After classes ended, I went to the café alone. We sat together, and between a little chat and laughter, we ordered two chicken sandwiches. That meeting marked the beginning of a story filled with passion and challenges."

She was silent for a few moments and continued:

He was, and still is, a part of a past I will never forget as long as I live, and he will stay with me in spirit as I start a new chapter. Today, I want to live only for myself.

She sipped her warm tea and said to Howaida:

"My friend, every time I see you, I realize I am still living in the beautiful past I shared with you. May God protect you."

Everyone ended the wonderful night wishing each other sweet dreams. Before Nahla went to sleep, she wrote in her diary:

"It was a wonderful day. I met friends who are close to my soul. I am certain that distance will not separate us, as loyal hearts always find a way to meet. It may hurt us that the next meeting may be delayed, but loyalty keeps our hearts close, no matter how far apart we are."

On the last day before traveling, the fun trio: Nahla, Alaa, and Howaida, went out early in the morning to enjoy every moment. They had breakfast in Sharjah, then had lunch at an Iraqi restaurant in Dubai, and concluded the day with a visit to Global Village in Dubai in the afternoon.

They had an unforgettable time and returned in the evening exhausted, but carrying with them the most beautiful memories of their lives. After that, they went to sleep so that Nahla could prepare for a long journey.

(2)
The Last Goodbye

Silence is sometimes the only language that tired hearts understand

At eleven o'clock at night on July 14, 2015, Alaa and Howaida bid farewell to their friend Nahla at the airport gate. In a moment of farewell filled with sadness, Alaa stood next to Nahla, her eyes brimming with tears, while

Howaida held Nahla's hands, and a silence heavy with emotions fell over everyone. Those moments encapsulated a long lifetime of friendship, dreams, and unforgettable memories. Time passed quickly as if it weren't enough to tell all the stories that still reside in their hearts.

On their way to the baggage claim office, silence reigned, and words seemed incapable of expression, as if everyone knew that no words would be enough.

Only the eyes spoke, expressing what words could not. When they completed the required procedures, they had time, so everyone sat in the cafeteria. Each of them tried to find appropriate words to commemorate the moment, but their feelings were intertwined, and they all came out with nothing but silent glances that reflected the pain of separation.

After a long silence, broken by the echo of the final moments, Alaa held Nahla's hand tenderly and said with a smile mixed with tears:

"Nahla, you look so beautiful and elegant today, as always. Honestly... I can't imagine the days to come without you."

Nahla smiled a weak smile, reflecting the exhaustion of her soul, and said:

"I feel my strength fading, Alaa. I don't know if I'll be able to continue living abroad alone."

Howayda, with sincere faith in her friend, took the initiative and said confidently:

"No, you are strong, Nahla. You will overcome this, and you will succeed in everything you have planned. This is not a farewell, but a new beginning for your life."

Despite the sadness that gripped her, Nahla felt a spark of strength creep into her heart. Alaa and Howayda's words were like a light illuminating her dark path, a promise that the dreams they shared would live on and one day come true.

Nahla sighed deeply and said in a voice filled with doubt:

"Will I be able to get rid of this pain that has weighed down my heart? I feel like I'm carrying the weight of the entire world on my shoulders."

Alaa answered her tenderly, her voice sincere:

"Yes, you will, Nahla, but only if you truly want it. Now you have freedom in every sense of the word. This is the time to focus on yourself, on what you truly want."

Nahla tried to gather her strength and asked in a choked-up voice:

"And what about my mother? She'll call me and try to convince me to come back. How can I face her?"

Howayda smiled, that smile that always filled her with reassurance, and said:

"Tell her that when you settle down, you'll invite her to visit, or maybe Omar will invite her to visit you and be near you. That isn't a separation, but a step toward building a better future. Tell her that you need this time to rediscover yourself and renew your energy. Now is your time, Nahla."

For the first time in a long time, Nahla felt safe, as if Alaa and Howayda's words were a key to unlocking her burdened heart. Everyone was silent for a moment, tears welling in their eyes, each one knowing that this farewell might be the most difficult of her life. Suddenly, as if Howayda remembered something, she said:

"Nahla, do you remember the nursing course we took together after graduation? How dedicated and hardworking you were."

Everyone laughed together, recalling those beautiful memories. Nahla smiled:

"Yes, I remember. But why did I remember it now?" Howayda answered enthusiastically:

"Because I think you could use that experience now. You could apply for a job in a nursing home or hospital; it would be a good step to starting a new life."

The thought lit up Nahla's face as if she saw a glimmer of hope at the end of the tunnel. She said enthusiastically:

"I think you're right. It might be a good opportunity to find a job."

As the inevitable farewell approached, tears streamed from their eyes uncontrollably. Each tried to show the other her strength, but separation was stronger than anything. When it came to enter the waiting room, Alaa held Nahla's hand tightly, as if afraid to let her go, and said in a voice choked with tears,

My beloved sister, who has accompanied me my entire life, I entrust you to God, who never loses deposits. Always remember that my home is your home, and that you are never alone.

After that, Howaida grabbed Nahla's hands and hugged her tightly, urging her not to hesitate to call them if she needed anything. They embraced one last time, as Nahla slipped from Alaa and Howaida's arms, carrying her words like a safety talisman in her heart. Those words were the last things Nahla heard before she left, and the last things she had left of her homeland and her friends. A farewell filled with love, despite the pain and tears, and a promise that dreams, no matter how far apart, would one day bring them together.

Chapter Twelve

(1)
Emigration... A New Chapter

Every farewell is another beginning. We don't know where it will take us, but it always teaches us something about ourselves.

The moment the door of the plane to London closed, Nahla felt as if she was turning a page in her life, perhaps an entire book, filled with small losses and simple victories, disappointments, dreams, sorrows, and incomplete joys. Fifty years have passed, during which she has lived almost everything, but now she has decided to start over. She had been preparing herself for this step for three years, but the final farewell was harder than she expected.

She sat in her window seat, staring at the clouds as she prepared herself for the long journey, not just between continents, but toward a known-unknown future.

Before the plane took off, she picked up her phone and called her mother:

"Mom, I'm on the plane now."

'May God protect you, my daughter. I entrust you to God, who never loses trust. Don't forget to send me a message or call as soon as you arrive. I'll be worried until you reassure me.'

"Of course, I promise you. I love you."

Her mother wished her luck and a successful trip. Her words were warm, but her voice sounded a little broken, as if she was trying to suppress her emotions to appear strong in front of her daughter. Minutes before the plane took off, while the young flight attendant, dressed in a navy-blue uniform adorned with a red, blue, and white scarf, was checking that her seatbelts were fastened, Nahla turned to hear a woman reciting the prayer for travel. She smiled and asked:

"Are you Iraqi?"

The woman laughed and replied with a smile:

"Yes, I am Iraqi. Thank God, I found a travel companion to accompany me on the long journey."

She replied:

"I am Nahla, Iraqi too."

With a transparent smile, she replied:

"I'm Iqbal..."

Nahla's expression indicated fatigue, so Iqbal asked her: "Are you okay?"

Nahla replied with a sigh and a sad smile:

"Yes, I'm fine, but now I've parted ways with my dearest loved ones. I don't know if I'll ever see them again."

The curiosity of the dark-skinned woman in her fifties, with her round, full face, sultry eyes, and jet-black hair tied back, grew stronger. She gently asked another question:

"Where are you going?"

"I'm traveling to Canada, but I have an eight-hour transit at Heathrow Airport."

The woman smiled, wrapping her brown shawl around her shoulders, and said:

"Masha 'Allah, a long trip. I'm going to visit my daughter, who lives in London."

Nahla smiled, feeling a sense of relief in the conversation with Iqbal:

"It's a pleasure to meet you, Iqbal. It seems that fate wanted to give me a travel companion on this journey."

"I'm also happy to meet you, Nahla. Tell me, are you from Baghdad?" Nahla replied enthusiastically:

"Yes, I was born and raised in Adhamiya." Iqbal was excited and said eagerly:

"Ah, Baghdad, my love, what a city full of history and beauty. I'm also from Baghdad, a resident of Kadhimiya, but I've lived in the UAE for many years."

Nahla agreed with the woman:

"That's true. The UAE is a wonderful country full of vitality and diversity. I, too, have lived in the UAE for twenty years."

Iqbal:

"Life is beautiful in the UAE, full of opportunities, but Baghdad will always be in my heart."

The two women exchanged conversations as if they were old friends, talking about Baghdad and sewing, as well as humanitarian work, the years that had passed, and longing for the streets and markets that now exist only in memory. When Iqbal asked Nahla about her marital status, she answered in a choked-up voice: "I was engaged to an officer in the Iraqi army. We were about to get married... but a few months before our wedding, he was martyred in the First Qadisiyah War, in the Basra sector."

She was silent for a moment, then continued:

"Since then, I have vowed to live faithfully to his love. Every charitable act I have done has been motivated by the feeling that he is still with me."

Iqbal looked at her with tears in her eyes:

"I'm sorry... I didn't know." Nahla replied with a sad smile:

"It's okay. This is my life, and I live it every day, trying to find happiness in the rest of my life."

They did not pause throughout the journey. They discussed all topics, and at one point, Iqbal asked Nahla about sewing:

"Do you consider sewing your hobby? And how did it start?" Nahla replied with a smile mixed with sadness and nostalgia:

"When I was twenty, I was invited to a friend's birthday party, and I didn't have a suitable dress. I borrowed my sister's dress without her permission. When I returned home, she greeted me in a state of extreme anger and rage. I tried to justify my position, but she wouldn't listen. In her moment of anger, she tore the dress while I was still wearing it. I cried a lot."

Nahla sighed, looked as if she were seeing a scene unfold before her, and continued:

"A few days later, I was visiting my friend, whose mother is a skilled seamstress. I told her about the dress, and after seeing it, she told me it couldn't be fixed as it was, but she could alter it. I drew a design, and she succeeded in making it happen. That day marked the beginning of my journey with sewing. I began buying used clothes from the flea market, washing them, and redesigning them. It wasn't a professional design, but rather a way of repairing damaged items into something beautiful."

Then she laughed lightly and continued:

"This is how my story with fashion design began. As they say, every cloud has a silver lining."

While the plane was still flying quietly among the white clouds, Iqbal felt she had found a soulmate on this journey.

She gently took Nahla's hand and said:

"Nahla, would you accept us being more than just flying companions? Two friends, or even two sisters?"

Nahla replied tenderly:

"Of course, Iqbal. I feel comfortable with you. It's like we've known each other for a long time."

Iqbal laughed, paused for a few moments, and then continued, saying:

"Do you know, Nahla? Yesterday, I was at Global Village in Dubai with my son, his wife, and my grandson. My grandson rode the Ferris wheel. I wished I could have been with him, but I was afraid to ride it and later regretted it. Now I'm thinking of asking my daughter in London to go to the amusement park so I can try it."

Nahla laughed too:

"Yesterday, my friends and I were at Al Qasba in Sharjah, and we rode the Ferris wheel. I don't know why. We felt like high school girls."

Iqbal responded with a warm smile, "Memories have their magic. They always take us back to the places that embraced our souls."

Nahla said thoughtfully:

"When I visit a place far from Baghdad and feel it resembles it, I immediately connect to it. That's how I feel when I visit Sharjah."

The conversation between Iqbal and Nahla seemed to take on a deeper tone, so Iqbal asked Nahla:

"What did you do in the Emirates?"

Nahla smiled and answered:

"I used to work in a care home for people with special needs, and in addition, I used to practice my hobby of sewing. I have a small sewing workshop at home, where I design and sew children's clothes and sometimes abayas."

Iqbal was impressed by her response and said:

"Masha'Allah, your work is truly special," Nahla replied with a wide smile:

"I love my work very much. It reminds me of what I used to do when I was in Baghdad. There, I worked with a group of women who visited needy families and took care of their children. We also had a sewing workshop where we designed and sewed clothes for boys, girls, and all family members."

Iqbal was surprised and asked her:

"Where did you live in Baghdad?" Nahla answered:

"I told you, I was living in Adhamiya, but I used to go with associations interested in charitable work to remote villages, and we used to care for families with limited income in the suburbs of Baghdad as well as the villages and rural areas.

"This humanitarian work didn't just bring us a small salary, but it meant a lot to me. In addition, I was working as a clerk at a high school, which added a lot of valuable experience.? Iqbal smiled and said:

"Your story is truly inspiring, Nahla. It seems you live with a passion for doing good."

A moment of silence fell between them. Iqbal's gaze was filled with wonder and wonder, as if she was trying to understand more about Nahla's life. She asked:

"And did your family support you after your fiancé was martyred?" "I have a feeling they supported you so you could get back on your feet and move on with your life."

Nahla smiled and said:

"My family?"

She was silent for a few moments, then replied in a voice filled with pain: "Of course, as a family, they offered him whatever support they could."

As the plane flew quietly among the white clouds, the sky outside the window seemed like another world full of secrets. Iqbal was overwhelmed with mixed feelings of nostalgia and anticipation as she looked at Nahla sitting next to her. Although they had only known each other for a few hours, Iqbal sensed a hidden bond between them, as if fate had wanted them to meet on this flight.

(2)
Nostalgia for the Past

Home is not the place where we live, but rather memories that reside with us wherever we go.

The plane was quietly making its way above the clouds, while the warm cabin lights reflected on the faces of Iqbal and Nahla sitting side by side.

At that moment, the flight attendant approached with a calm smile, carrying the dinner meals, interrupting a conversation that flowed between them like a thread of rare warmth.

Iqbal took her plate and smiled at Nahla, as if they had a silent agreement that their conversation wasn't over, but had just begun. We began to eat to the faint rhythm of the plane's engines, when Nahla broke the silence, in a soft but gently curious voice.

"Why are you traveling alone, and where is your husband?"

Iqbal stopped cutting the food and raised her eyes toward the ceiling of the plane, as if delving into a memory box that was rarely opened. Moments of silence passed, heavy as clouds behind the windows, before she spoke in a low, melancholy voice:

"I am a widow... I lost my husband in 2004, on a dark morning after the occupation of Iraq."

Nahla's face showed surprise, but she didn't interrupt. Iqbal continued, her eyes sunken into the past:

"My husband and I owned an engineering office in Mansour. On the morning of April 3, he left for work as usual, and moments after, a motorcycle drove past our house, carrying two masked men who opened fire on him outside the door. I didn't realize at the time how many bullets had struck his heart and pierced his lungs. I just saw him fall in front of me... The world went black in my eyes at that moment, and everything after that became a blur."

Her tears flowed silently, as if they were the tears that always find their way to every memory. Then she added:

"A few days before, we had received a threatening letter with a bullet, stating that we had to leave our home and move out within three days. We notified the police, and they told us not to worry, but we were truly alone. Less than a week later, I became a widow."

Iqbal put the fork aside and wiped her tears with a small handkerchief from her bag. Nahla listened intently, a tear involuntarily slipping from her eye.

The widow continued, saying:

"After the funeral, I took my children and traveled to Erbil, where we stayed for several months. During that time, my family covered the cost of selling the house and everything else. Then I got a visa to the UAE and began to make my way back to Sharjah. I worked as an engineer in an engineering office and raised my children until they grew up and got married. It wasn't easy... but that's life. It didn't give us everything we hoped for, but praise and thanks be to God for everything."

She sighed, as if the weight of years had just lifted, then smiled calmly:

"My husband has never left me. I see him in my children's eyes, in the sound of my grandchildren laughing. He lives inside me to this day."

Nahla gently reached out and patted Iqbal's hand:

"I'm sorry... I didn't mean to open your wound."

Iqbal smiled, a smile that held the maturity of pain and the kindness of those reconciled to longing, and added:

"It's okay, my dear. Pain doesn't mean we're not living. It means we loved truly, and perhaps that's why I felt close to you when you told me about your martyred fiancé, Nidal. We know each other from the depths of pain, not from the surface of words."

A soft silence fell, befitting a sky filled with postponed stories. Then Nahla whispered, trying to illuminate some of the lightness of the moment:

"Let's finish dinner before it gets cold... We don't want to lose its flavor either."

They laughed together, a laugh that resembled the calm after a storm, as if the chance of sharing a seat wasn't random, but rather a fate written in the unseen. After dinner, Nahla and Iqbal didn't remain silent for a moment, as if the doors of the past had opened for them to remember all the beautiful things they shared, especially their memories of beloved Baghdad. As they sipped tea, Nahla brought up an interesting topic and said to Iqbal:

"Shall I tell you something? My school was in Kadhimiya, and I lived in

Adhamiya. The most beautiful thing for me was crossing the Imam's Bridge on foot with my schoolmates and lifelong companions. We enjoyed crossing the bridge more than we enjoyed going to school."

Iqbal laughed and said:

"What a coincidence! Did you know that I also used to cross the Imam's Bridge on foot? But that was to get to the bus stop that would take me to the College of Engineering in Bab al-Mu'adham. As I told you, I live in

Kadhimiya has always held a special charm for me, with its old alleys and its religious and historical spirit. I felt a sense of serenity every time I crossed the bridge, and I saw the domes of Imam Al-Kadhim (peace be upon him) looming on the horizon."

Nahla smiled and said:

"Didn't I tell you that we have a lot in common?" Iqbal then continued:

"Not only that, but I was also training in an engineering office on Al-Dhabat Street in Adhamiya, an area that was and still is full of life and activity. I used to work there part-time because I used to study in the morning, and in the evening I would go to the engineering office to practice and at the same time work my husband, may God have mercy on him, he was the owner of the engineering office before he transferred him to Al-Mansour after our marriage, and from there our beautiful love story began when I graduated from university, he proposed to me and we got married."

Nahla replied with a smile:

"How beautiful is the love relationship that results from marriage and children, that immortalize these beautiful memories. It is truly wellness for the heart and soul."

Their conversation continued, filled with beautiful memories of Adhamiya and Kadhimiya, and of Baghdad, which holds within it tales of the past, secrets of love, and the beauty and splendor of the past. There were still two hours left to reach London, where the plane would land at Heathrow Airport. Iqbal looked at Nahla with a warm smile and asked:

"Nahla, what will you do during the wait? You will have eight hours until your flight to Toronto takes off."

Nahla answered, looking out the window at the sky:

"I don't think it will be long. I'll collect my bags first, then go to the cafeteria for lunch. After that, I'll go to the duty-free shop to buy a gift for my brother Omar, who will meet me upon my arrival in Toronto. After that, I'll head to the waiting lounge until it's time to head to the airline office to prepare for the flight."

Iqbal enthusiastically suggested:

"Would you like me to stay with you?" Nahla responded gently:

"No, please don't miss the most beautiful moments between you, your daughter, and your grandchildren. Time will fly by between picking up our bags, eating lunch, and packing our bags in preparation for the next trip."

Iqbal smiled with love and agreed, saying:

"Okay, you're right, Nahla. I'll do what you say."

Both exchanged phone numbers, each carrying mixed feelings of joy and longing in her heart. When the plane landed at Heathrow Airport, each of them bid the other farewell with a warm embrace. It was a heartfelt farewell full of hope, with a strong feeling in each of their hearts that this would not be the last farewell, but rather the beginning of a new friendship and stories waiting to be told.

Chapter Thirteen

(1)
Fate's Surprises

Memories don't die, but they subside when we learn to live in spite of them.

Nahla finished her lunch at a small table overlooking the wide corridor of the Heathrow Airport cafeteria, where the aromas of roasting coffee mingled with the scent of curry and chips. The sounds of spoons and plates clinked softly, while flight announcements played from the loudspeakers like incessant background music. Behind the wide glass, planes were lined up like metal birds preparing for flight, and light rain traced diagonal lines on the wet floor.

She wiped her lips with a napkin, stood up, straightened her jacket, and made her way through the crowd toward the baggage claim office.

Travelers hurried around her, luggage dragging, children running, and multiple dialects intermingling like a small city of passersby.

Since there was still time, she headed to the duty-free shop. Its bright lights and colorful shelves caught her eye, and she paused in front of the perfume corner, where scents mingled: jasmine, amber, and a light hint of vanilla. Amidst the carefully arranged perfume bottles and chocolate boxes, she searched for a gift for her brother Omar, who had promised to be the first to hug her when she arrived in Toronto.

As she browsed the duty-free shops, her attention was drawn to a turquoise dress with a simple design. Something about it suddenly brought back a painful memory of her time with her sister Nadine. She paused in front of it for a long time, touching it with her hand, as if trying to recall a part of her past she had never been able to forget.

She recalled her middle school days, when she was in the fourth grade of high school, at the age of fifteen. Her school organized a trip to a tourist town near her hometown.

Nahla owned a limited number of simple clothes, some of which were unsuitable for going out with her friends. So, she asked her sister, Nadine, who was ten years older than her, to lend her a dress to wear on the school trip. Nadine vehemently refused, arguing that the dress might get ruined.

She told her in a bullying tone:

"This dress doesn't suit you because it's too expensive."

Nahla had no choice but to wear a skirt that was too tight for her and an old shirt. During the trip, the zipper on her skirt came undone. She and her friends searched for a needle and thread to fix it and continued on with the trip, but her heart was heavy with embarrassment and bitterness. She completed the day with a broken joy, the painful memories still fresh in her mind.

Nahla left the dress and walked quietly to another section of the duty-free shop. She chose a winter sweater and a bottle of perfume as gifts for her brother Omar and his wife and asked the employee to wrap them carefully. Then she returned to the waiting lounge, waiting for the call to board the plane. The flight would be long, eight hours nonstop to Toronto, and as she looked at the clock, she thought about how many memories a dress could awaken, but she decided to leave the past where it was, carrying only what she needed for the future.

She waited a long time before heading to her plane after the call that filled the airport lounges for passengers traveling to Toronto. She completed the boarding procedures.

She soon sat in her seat by the window, contemplating the white clouds in the blue sky. She wondered silently:

"I wonder what fate has in store for me there? How will my life be in a strange country where I know no one except my brother Omar and his family? Will I be able to rebuild myself?"

Many questions ran through her mind, to which she found no answers, as the plane prepared for takeoff. With the captain's call, Nahla felt a strange mixture of dread, joy, and pain. She knew that this moment meant that she was finally separated from her family, leaving behind everything she knew and everyone she loved. She couldn't pinpoint the emotion that was throbbing inside her, but her heart was groaning with longing, fear, and hope, as the plane took off toward a new sky and a new life awaiting her, far from everything familiar.

Feelings of anxiety slowly began to creep into Nahla's depths. She felt as though her decision to travel to Canada might be a grave mistake. She had a tourist visa for Greece, which was her second option if she didn't succeed in obtaining a Canadian visa. Her thoughts revolved around the possibility that Greece, and specifically the city of Patra, might be a better start for her new life. Her relatives lived there, and she had many childhood memories, when she accompanied her late father and mother there when he was sent on a six-month work assignment. She studied at the Arab Expatriates School, where she was in the fifth grade. There, she fell in love with life in Greece, and to this day, she still remembers the most beautiful moments of her childhood in Patra.

But fate took a different course, as she obtained a Canadian visa and decided to make her way to Canada. The decision was difficult and decisive, and there was no turning back after being separated from her family. She told herself:

"The most important thing is that I paid three months' rent for a room and bathroom in a shared accommodation with a Canadian family in advance, which meant I was guaranteed a place to stay from day one in Toronto. In addition, I have enough money to cover my daily needs and transportation, which gives me enough time to explore the place and look for work."

She asked herself:

"Why the fear? Aren't we the ones who create the future? God will guide me in my steps, and if I fail here, I will look for new opportunities elsewhere."

With these thoughts, Nahla broke the state of anxiety that had controlled her. She grabbed a book and began reading to occupy herself to pass the time. She alternated between reading, sleeping, and eating, until the hours passed and she found herself at Toronto Airport, where the plane landed at exactly eleven o'clock in the morning.

(2)
New Beginning

Sometimes, we don't choose exile... we choose ourselves, and we leave behind everything we love so that we don't lose what we could be.

When Nahla arrived at Toronto Airport, she was welcomed by her brother Omar, his wife, and his children. They welcomed her with a warm smile and great longing. They hugged her warmly, and her brother said:

"My dear Nahla, thank God you are safe. You have finally arrived."

The meeting was warm and full of nostalgia. Everyone headed to Omar's house in Mississauga, where her brother told her that she would be staying with them until the university registration process was complete, and also to check on her in her new housing.

Despite Omar's repeated insistence that she would live with them; Nahla convinced him that she wanted to feel some independence.

In any case, her new housing wasn't far from them; it was close to the university and only twenty minutes from her residence. In the end, Omar acquiesced to her decision.

Nahla never stopped communicating with her mother. She calls her daily, and Omar sometimes joins the call, which made her mother feel comfortable and reassured. After several days of outings, completing her paperwork, and enrolling in university, Omar and his wife took her to her friend Maha's house in Toronto. She and her husband welcomed them warmly. Maha insisted on hosting them, but after two hours of hosting them, Nahla asked Maha to accompany her to see her new residence.

Despite Maha's insistence that she stay with her tonight and accompany her to her new residence the next day, Nahla insisted and said:

"Thank you very much, my friend, for the invitation, but I am eager to see my residence first. I want to pack my bags and get to know the family I will be living with. After that, I would be very happy to visit you in the evening."

Maha welcomed the idea without hesitation and said:

"Of course, no problem at all. In fact, my house is very close to your residence, just one street separates them, we can walk to it easily."

Maha then began sharing some details about the family that would be hosting Nahla, saying:

"The family is very nice. They consist of a mother, a father, and four children, but three of them are married and living outside the home. They only have their youngest daughter, an eleventh-grade student, who still lives with them.

I think you'll like the location; it's very close to the bus station, making it easy to get around."

Nahla felt comfortable and reassured as Maha continued talking. She paused for a moment, then said:

"In my opinion, rest and organize your things in your new home. In the evening, I'll visit you again to take you to my house. We'll all have dinner with my husband and children so you can get to know them."

Nahla felt warmed and encouraged by Maha's words, and replied enthusiastically:

"That's a great idea. I'd love to meet your family." When Nahla, her brother Omar, his wife, and Maha arrived at the Canadian family's home, she felt a wave of reassurance and relief. Laura, the owner of the house, welcomed her warmly.

The house was warm and comfortable, and when she entered her own room, she felt for the first time that she truly owned something of her own. This room, for which she had paid rent, was her new kingdom.

She whispered to herself with a small smile:

"This is the beginning... a completely new beginning."

Nahla bid farewell to her brother and his wife with love after they checked on her and her apartment. He promised to visit her at the end of the following week. That evening, Maha came to visit Nahla, looking concerned and eager to check on her. She knocked gently on the door, and when Nahla opened it, Maha smiled and asked:

"How are you, Nahla? Are you comfortable in the apartment? Is it suitable for you?"

Nahla replied with a calm smile:

"Yes, praise be to God, the place is very comfortable, and the family seems nice."

Maha was silent for a moment and said:

"I'll be honest with you. I've known this family for a while, and they're good people, but they have a strange quality for us Arabs, they love privacy and don't tend to mingle with others quickly. It takes time for them to open up to you."

Nahla interrupted her with a reassuring smile and said:

"Don't worry. I also like privacy, and I don't like others interfering in my private life. In fact, I spoke with Laura, the owner of the house, and she was very kind. She gave me instructions on how to use the stove and the washing machine, and told me that I couldn't host strangers, except for you and my brother Omar. I welcomed and accepted her instructions completely."

Maha smiled with relief and said:

"That's good. I think you'll get used to the place quickly. Now, let's go to my house. Today you are an honored guest at our table."

Before she was about to leave, Nahla gently stopped Maha and said:

"Maha, before we leave, I would like to give you this gift. I hope you like it and that it will reflect your status with me."

Maha looked at the gift in genuine surprise and said: "Why did you bother? There was no need for it." Nahla replied with a warm smile:

"This is a very modest gift, but it's an expression of my gratitude and appreciation. You've helped me a lot... Also, I'd like to give you the gift Alaa sent you."

Maha was deeply touched, and she hugged Nahla warmly, saying:

"It's enough for me that you're Alaa's friend. Now I feel as if Alaa is with me, but in person."

Nahla smiled, and felt a warm moment of familiarity and gratitude. Then they set off together to Maha's house, where an evening full of pleasure and enjoyment awaited them.

Chapter Fourteen

(1)
The alienation was not in the place, but in the beginning I was alone... but love opened a door for me that I did not expect.

Nahla arrived at her friend's house and walked down a brick path to the entrance, where Essam, Maha's husband, greeted her with a broad smile that filled his plump face, his white teeth shining amidst his tanned complexion. His sons, Kamel and Farouk, hovered around him. The house was simple, two-story, with a red-tiled roof and gray siding, like most houses. It stood on a corner where three roads intersected, and had a small garden and a covered garage in front of it.

The place was filled with the warm welcome offered by the family. Maha resembled a bee, going gracefully between the kitchen and the living room. She wore her long black hair high, highlighting her thin white neck on which sat a small, soft head, a delicate face, and hazel eyes.

Despite the wide, flowing dress, her grace was evident, especially as she and her children carried the lavish dinner plates she had prepared for the precious guest.

The lady of the house had laid out the most delicious Iraqi dishes, the favorites of the friend arriving from afar. The family sat around the table, chatting while Maha served everyone the food. The conversations around the delicious table alternated between stories of life in Canada and memories of the past in Baghdad. During dinner, Essam took the initiative to ask the guest:

"What are your plans to work here? Do you have a recommendation from anyone or an idea of what you want to do?"

Nahla replied after thinking for a while, saying:

"I definitely have plans, the most important of which is studying, as I will be joining university in a month and a half, God willing. As for work, I didn't think much about it and left it until I arrived. I have a certificate of experience from the Emirates working in centers for people with special needs. I am also a skilled seamstress, and I am good at designing children's clothes and abayas. I have a resume of my participation in several exhibitions. I am also a skilled cook."

Essam smiled kindly and said:

"I'll tell you frankly, here in Canada, you don't rely on Middle Eastern credentials. You must pass certain tests to obtain a work permit or license to practice the profession."

Nahla felt a bit worried and asked:

"Does that mean I'll need a long time to obtain my work permit?" Essam responded reassuringly:

"Not at all. To ease your worries, I have a suggestion. Tomorrow, you and Maha will go buy a Canadian phone number. I also have a friend who owns an Arabic products store who can hire you on an hourly basis. You won't need a bank account now, and he'll pay you $14 per hour. In the meantime, we'll submit your resume to various places, such as hospitals and health centers."

Nahla interrupted him anxiously:

"I have a Canadian number. My brother Omar bought it for me when I arrived in Toronto. But my question is, if I'm going to be working all day, how will I be able to study, search for jobs, and attend interviews?"

Maha intervened, saying:

"Don't worry. The Arab store is open from 8 a.m. to 8 p.m., and they have a shift schedule, so you can work in the evening and go to university in the morning."

Nahla felt relieved and grateful to Essam and Maha for their support, before their son Farouk interrupted her encouragingly:

"Aunt Nahla, if you'd like, I can help you rewrite your resume. A resume here in Canada is completely different from the Middle East, and you also need to include a cover letter, which varies depending on the employer."

Nahla listened attentively and thanked him warmly, saying:

"Tomorrow morning, God willing, I'll give your mother my papers so she can deliver them to you."

Farouk responded enthusiastically:

"Great! And I'll add your Canadian phone number to your resume, too."

Nahla felt internally happy to be supported by Maha's family, but at the same time, she was also a little apprehensive.

This new path was full of challenges, and for the first time, she was walking it alone, fully responsible for her decisions. In a moment of silence, Maha interrupted her with a smile and asked:

"Would you like tea or coffee after dinner?"

Nahla chose coffee, and they sat in the garden, enjoying the calm night air. July was mild after a harsh polar winter.

Maha asked curiously:

"Do you have internet access, or would you like me to give you the password?"

Nahla then remembered that she hadn't contacted her mother or her friend Alaa. She smiled and said:

"Thanks, I really need it. I haven't contacted anyone."

She wrote a quick message to reassure her mother, and another to Alaa, telling her that she would call them the next morning, as the time difference prevented her from calling today. An hour later, Nahla excused herself to return to her apartment for a rest. Maha offered to drive her, but Nahla politely declined, saying:

"I don't want to tire you out. I've known the way, and it's easy."

Essam thanked her saying, "You are Maha's sister, and I am your brother. Don't hesitate to ask for any help you need."

Nahla smiled, bid farewell to them, and returned to her apartment feeling reassured. She said her prayers just before going to bed, hoping that tomorrow would be a successful start. Before going to sleep, she took out her diary and wrote:

"The road may be new and frightening, but the warmth of the hearts around me made the first step on it possible."

The next morning, Nahla woke up from a deep sleep with soft knocks on her door. Laura, the owner of the house, came to wake her up and invite her to breakfast. Nahla welcomed her kindly and asked her for a few minutes to get ready, take a shower, and change her clothes. When she finished, she found that Laura had prepared a breakfast table in the garden, welcoming her warmly. While eating breakfast, Laura asked Nahla if the food was suitable for her, and Nahla responded gratefully:

"Very good. I love eggs and cheese." Thank you so much for the invitation. Laura smiled and said:

"I'm so happy to have you with me, and I hope you achieve all your dreams."

Nahla thanked her again. Meanwhile, Maha arrived to take her to the Arabic Store, where they were scheduled to meet Essam. On their way, Nahla enjoyed the picturesque scenery, as most of the roads were lined with trees. She said to Maha with admiration:

"Mashallah, Canada has such a stunning nature." Maha agreed, replying:

"My dear, you haven't seen anything like Canada's beauty yet. The lakes and forests here are the most amazing. Did you know that behind Mrs. Laura's house, there is a forest and a small lake?"

Nahla was surprised and didn't ask more questions. Maha

continued the explanation:

"These forests are nature reserves, home to deer, squirrels, and even bears, and no one is allowed to disturb them. This weekend, I'll take you there, and you're going to have a wonderful time."

It wasn't long before they arrived at the Arabic store, where Essam was waiting for them. He introduced Nahla to the store owner and his wife. The store owner, Abu Hilal, agreed to let Nahla work the evening shift, which gave her enough time during the morning to study and look for another suitable job. They agreed that she would start work the next day.

After they left, Issam suggested a drive to Nahla to show her around the city. On the way, Maha asked:

"What would you like for lunch today? Do you have anything in mind, or should Issam and I choose for you?"

She replied shyly:

"Really, this is too much for me." Maha laughed and said:

"My dear, we haven't done anything. Tomorrow, God willing, you'll start your job, and we won't see you again until the weekend."

Nahla delegated the decision to them, and Issam told her they would eat fish. Today was Wednesday, and fish is a tradition in Baghdad, where they believe fish brings prosperity. Everyone laughed and agreed. After a pleasant stroll through the streets of Toronto, they concluded their day with a delicious fish meal at a restaurant. Time passed quickly, and no one realized it had passed until Nahla looked at the clock and said in surprise, "It's 5:00 PM."

Maha then asked:

"What do you have on your schedule now?" You will come home with me, and we will have tea together, right?

She responded kindly:

"Please allow me to return to the dorm. I haven't packed my bag yet, and I haven't explored the room thoroughly. I also want to call my mother and sister before it's midnight there. Don't forget the time difference."

Maha agreed with a gentle nod, and before Nahla got out of the car, she handed Amal her certificate and CV to deliver to her son Farouk. Before that, she asked:

"How can I buy a kettle?"

Maha interrupted her again enthusiastically, saying:

"I'll send you one with a box of tea bags with Farouk as soon as I get home." Despite Nahla's objections, Maha insisted:

"Trust me, this kettle is something I've never used before, and I have two. You can borrow one and return it when you don't need it."

Nahla thanked her warmly, then said goodbye and went to her room to rest.

As soon as she threw herself onto the bed, she felt exhausted. She was exhausted from the trip. After an hour of rest, she slowly got up and started packing her bag, exploring the room as if she was seeing it for the first time.

For the first time, the room was simple and comfortable, painted in a light beige color. It contained a single bed, next to a small closet with light brown wooden drawers, a small lamp above it, and a small white refrigerator for storing food. To the side, she found a small closet and a small bathroom next to it. She examined the room carefully and said:

"I need a reading table and a chair."

In a moment, Nahla focused her gaze on the window overlooking the garden. The scene was magical, with the sky overcast, as if rain were about to fall at any moment. After she finished organizing her things, she sat down on the bed in a relaxed position and called her mother. As soon as her mother answered, the girl couldn't stop her tears from falling, but her mother was quick to respond with warm words:

"Nahla, my love, how are you, my sweetheart?"

Nahla replied in a tired voice:

"Praise be to God, Mom, I'm fine. Don't worry. Reassure me. How are you and your health?"

Her mother responded tenderly:

"Are you comfortable? If you want to come back, I'd be happy."

Nahla quickly interrupted her:

"Have Jumana and Nadine arrived?" Her mother answered:

"Yes, and they want to talk to you, and Adhraa too."

Nahla agreed enthusiastically and spoke with them, full of affection and good wishes for her new journey. Adhraa ended the call, and their conversation was not without tears and affection. Before the call ended, Nahla said to Adhraa:

"If you would like to call me later, get my number from my mother. Now, let me go, I am very tired and want to sleep."

She ended the call, but this time she felt something different inside her. There was no tension like she usually did when talking to her sisters.

Rather, there was a strange sensation that mixed psychological comfort, independence, and nostalgia; a feeling that a new phase had begun in her life, and that she was beginning to discover her inner strength and her readiness to face challenges with confidence and calm.

(2)
And the Journey Began

With every beginning far from home, a new part of us is born... nourished by nostalgia, grows with willpower, and blossoms when we believe that we deserve the life we dream of.

As night fell, Nahla felt extremely tired and sleepy, so she fell into a deep sleep. She woke up in the morning to the sound of birds chirping as they visited the maple tree near her window. Her room overlooked an enchanting garden, where the sparkling leaves of the apple tree danced in the morning sun. At first, she didn't know what kind of maple tree it was, but with time, she discovered that it was Canada's national symbol, adorning the Canadian flag with its distinctive red symbol. This tree, which changes color with the seasons, was also the source of the delicious maple honey that Canadians adored and considered an integral part of their diet and traditions.

Nahla opened her window wide and inhaled the fresh air, which was mingled with the scent of pristine nature and the scent of dew-drenched soil. The gentle breeze caressed her cheeks, bringing a sense of inner peace, as if nature itself were welcoming her to a new day. As she sat down to eat her simple breakfast, she decided to check her email.

A broad smile spread across her face when she saw a message from the university welcoming her. The message also included the schedule of courses she would begin studying. Nahla felt a wave of joy and reassurance, as if the door of hope was slowly opening before her. She began thinking about all the new opportunities that might soon present themselves. Suddenly, her phone rang, and Maha was eagerly on the other end. Nahla rushed to tell her the good news, to which Maha replied happily:

"That's wonderful, Nahla, and even more wonderful is that today is your first day at work. Do you want me to give you a ride?"

Nahla smiled and said with determination:

"Thank you, but I want to be independent. I want to explore the city and learn how to use public transportation."

Maha liked the idea and replied;

"Excellent idea. I'll accompany you today just to explain how to use the public transportation app and find the correct bus times and number. I'll arrive at 12:00."

At 12:00, Maha arrived at Nahla's house, and they went together to the bus station. She had downloaded the public transportation app on her expat friend's phone, and she guided her on how to search for schedules and bus numbers. The journey took about twenty minutes to reach "The Arab Shop," the store run by Abu Hilal and his wife, Umm Hilal. The store specialized in selling Middle Eastern groceries, with a special section for fresh vegetables and halal-slaughtered meat.

When Nahla arrived, Abu Hilal and his wife warmly welcomed her. She felt a little nervous, but she was optimistic that this day would be a new beginning. Abu Hilal and his wife began explaining the details of the job.

Nahla's tasks included arranging the merchandise on the shelves, organizing the fruits and vegetables, and ensuring the cleanliness of the display in the vegetable section. Umm Hilal devoted time to teaching her how to use the accounting machine and manage daily transactions.

Although Nahla was new to this type of work, she learned quickly and gradually began to feel comfortable. There weren't many customers at first, which gave her the opportunity to practice and adjust without pressure.

However, she was hesitant to use the cash register and asked her employer to refrain from using it for a while. Soon, a customer came in looking for ingredients to prepare a traditional Middle Eastern meal. Nahla asked Abu Hilal about the best options, and he explained how to choose the right spices and meats. This experience was the perfect opportunity for her to learn how to deal with customers in a professional and friendly manner.

The day passed quickly, and she began to master the daily tasks more quickly. She found herself enjoying chatting with Umm Hilal. She felt like part of a small family, and this sense of belonging boosted her confidence. When the clock struck eight, her first workday came to an end. The young woman was physically exhausted, but she was filled with joy at her accomplishments. She left the shop full of positivity and headed toward the bus station with greater confidence after such a productive day.

That evening, when Maha returned to check on her friend, she called her. The friend enthusiastically shared the details of her day, talking about the clients and the situations she'd encountered, and how she'd begun to feel comfortable at work. She was proud of her first step in her career,

Filled with optimism for what the future might hold, Nahla began her conversation with Maha, brimming with happiness, saying eagerly:

"I can't describe how happy I am, my friend. I never imagined something like this would happen to me while I was abroad. Today, after I finished my work, Abu Hilal gave me my daily wage of $112."

When I told him I wanted to go shopping and would pay for it, he laughed and said:

"Your shopping today is a gift from me and Umm Hilal as a welcome. Take whatever you want and whatever you like."

Nahla added enthusiastically:

"His generosity has really taken me out. I tried to be modest and only took a little of what I needed, but Umm Hilal was attentive to what I was doing and insisted on adding more legumes and vegetables, and even lamb and chicken."

Nahla took a deep breath and continued:

"I told her it was too much, but she smiled and said, 'Consider it a gift for our acquaintance." Imagine, Maha, the bags were heavy, but I felt so light with joy. I can't describe how grateful I am for them and for you as well. You made me feel like I'm not alone here."

Maha replied:

"We haven't done anything worthy of thanks, my friend. As we say in Iraq: 'What good have you done purely for the sake of God, that He should reward you now, while you are in exile, far from all those you love?'"

Nahla's eyes welled with tears from her joy and her being moved by Maha's words. She felt the warmth of friendship and appreciation before they could even finish their conversation. Maha invited her friend to dinner, but Nahla politely excused herself, saying:

"Thank you. I have to do some shopping and prepare lunch for tomorrow. I feel like I need to go to bed early because I'm exhausted."

The two friends concluded the call by praying for each other and wishing each other sweet dreams. Nahla was motivated to organize her shopping, then prepared a light dinner and cooked lunch for the next day. Her day had been filled with emotions and accomplishments. By the end, she felt exhausted, so she went to bed early, feeling rested and content, bathed in a sea of gratitude for the people who had surrounded her with love and care during her time abroad.

When Nahla sat on her bed, she opened her bag to pull out her first paycheck in Canada: $112. She held it in her hand and felt a special warmth, as if she were holding a great accomplishment in her hands.

As she contemplated that moment, her memory took her back to Abu Dhabi, when she was working at a center for people with special needs. It was her first salary there, and it was three thousand dirhams. Although it was a modest sum, it meant a lot to her. She felt proud at the time and shared her joy with her mother and brother, Marwan, over her first salary. When she entered the house, her mother congratulated her, saying:

"Congratulations, my sweetheart. What will you do with your first salary?" Nahla responded with a broad smile:

"First, I'll buy a cell phone and contribute to the cost of living and pay for some of the household necessities."

Her sister, Adhraa, responded somewhat haughtily:

"You don't need to buy a cell phone. Your home phone will suffice. I also don't need your contributions. I can handle everything."

Nahla felt a bit angry at her sister's response, but her mother interrupted her with a question:

"What about your sister, Jumana, and your brother, Marwan? Are you thinking of sending them some money? They will be grateful."

Nahla replied:

"My salary isn't enough to send them money, in addition to covering our household expenses."

But her mother didn't listen to her response. Instead, she took half of her salary, then sent the money to Jumana and Adhraa. Two days later, she called them and said:

"This is from me and Adhraa."

Nahla looked at her mother angrily and asked:

"Why did you say it was from you and Adhraa? Why didn't you tell them the truth?"

Her mother calmly replied:

"Because they feel bad about you. If they knew you were the one who sent the money, they would reject it. Consider it a charity for the sake of God, for God knows what you do."

Her eyes welled with tears, and she felt that her joy at her first salary had been shattered. This wasn't the moment she had been waiting for. It was a moment of happiness mixed with disappointment. She came to her senses for a moment and said to herself:

"Oh night, be kind to me as you tinker with the contents of my memory. My heart has been exhausted by its weary past, and now it seeks rest, peace, and tranquility. Be fair to me, as I, in my lonely exile, gather myself and refine myself anew."

Nahla decided not to tell anyone and to save her wages, because she didn't know what the coming days held for her. Despite all those memories that stirred sadness in her, Nahla felt great joy. Her achievement today was different; it came from herself alone, without interference from anyone.

She was proud of what she had accomplished and of every step she had taken toward independence and self-reliance.

Chapter Fifteen

(1)
Niagara Falls

When alienation mixes with curiosity, courage is born in us that we don't know we have.

The days passed quickly until Nahla had spent a month in Toronto without her noticing. She didn't notice how quickly the days passed as she was busy between daily job interviews and her work at the store. The new life was full of challenges and opportunities, and time passed without her noticing. She only had a week left before she started university. One quiet weekend morning, Nahla woke up to the ringing of her phone, to find that Maha was calling.

After a short conversation about the situation and the news, Maha said excitedly:

"Nahla! How about a trip to Niagara Falls? It's not far from Toronto, about an hour and a half by car. It would be a great opportunity to relax and enjoy the beauty of nature."

Nahla hesitated. Her mind was heavy with the small mess she'd left behind at home, so she said gently:

"Thank you so much, Maha. I feel like I need to stay home, especially since I visited you the first week after arriving in Toronto with my brother Omar's family."

Maha didn't back down, insisting tenderly:

"It's been a month, Nahla, and you've been running nonstop. You won't be visiting again. You'll see her through different eyes, immersed in tranquility this time."

Her words were sure to awaken something dormant. Nahla felt a need to escape the frenetic pace of life, and she finally smiled:

"You've convinced me. When do we leave?" Maha responded enthusiastically:

"Great! I'll stop by tomorrow morning at 9:00. We'll have breakfast on the way, and we'll arrive at the falls by noon."

The next morning, she set off with Maha and her family toward the falls. On the way, nature opened up before her like a living oil painting. The wheat fields swayed in the breeze, and wind turbines towered above them like guardians of time.

Then came the apple and corn farms, potato fields, and apple orchards stretching out as if endlessly, creating a symphony of the earth's colors. As the car drove on, Nahla's spirit revived. As soon as the outskirts of Niagara City appeared, the scene was transformed into a crowd of tourists and a bridge crossing the river, marking a transparent border between Canada and the United States.

When they arrived in Niagara City, the scene suddenly changed. The city's tourist attractions began to appear, and the city was teeming with tourists from all over the world. Nahla was surprised to discover that Niagara City lies on the border with New York State. A bridge separating the Canadian and American cities of Niagara City allows pedestrians and vehicles to cross between Canada and New York. It is the Rainbow Bridge, a bridge over the roaring river, and a bridge that travelers cross, as if they were transported between two worlds separated only by the mist and spray of the waterfalls.

But the most beautiful thing was the participation of the two cities, the American and the Canadian, in this amazing natural masterpiece, Niagara Falls. After they approached the falls, Issam, Maha's husband, booked tickets to board the boat that takes visitors on a tour close to the falls. The boat sailed with them under the rushing falls, the water spray gently caressing their faces. The scene was amazing, beyond description, as if nature was washing away all their worries and fatigue. Nahla turned to her friend, her eyes shining:

"It was as if the water had washed away all the fatigue. Thank you, my friend."

This was not the end of the trip, but rather its beginning. Maha then led them to the historic power station near the falls, which has since been decommissioned and has become a popular tourist attraction. The station is located 180 feet underground and can be reached through a 4-kilometer tunnel. During the tour, Nahla discovered that the temperature inside the tunnel was as low as 15 degrees Celsius, which added an exciting aspect to the trip.

While wandering through the corridors of the old station, Nahla was truly amazed. The station, which was once a source of energy for the region, has now become a landmark that tells stories of human exploitation of nature to generate energy. Established in 1905, it used the hydraulic power generated by Niagara Falls to generate electricity. The station continued to operate until 2006, when it was closed for renovations. In 2016, a new station was opened on the same site.

The trip was an enjoyable and full adventure. With surprises, Nahla didn't feel the time pass. When they returned to Toronto that evening, she felt as if she was breathing for the first time since arriving in Canada.

She realized that balance comes not only from organization and duties, but from rare moments she seizes in time... listening to her heart, and she finds the way. Before she went to sleep, she opened her small notebook and wrote:

"Sometimes, we don't need to change our lives, we just need a quiet moment that makes us see them from a different angle."

(2)
On the Benches of Dream

It is not late for those who walk steadily towards the light

On her first day of college, Nahla woke up before sunrise. Her hands were trembling as she turned off the alarm, not because it was annoying, but because her heart woke her up every day to a different reality. This day, however, was something else... a deferred dream about to come true. It was her first day at college, at the age of fifty.

She stood in front of the mirror, contemplating her face, which bore the faint lines of wrinkles of time, a silent signature of years of sacrifice and patience. With her fingertips, she smoothed the strands of hair that fell over her shoulders, took a deep breath, and then said in a low voice, as if to reassure her trembling heart:

"I am starting now."

She opened her closet and carefully chose what was appropriate for this different day: gray pants, a white blouse, a black jacket, and a red scarf that she wrapped around her neck as a touch of life. She quickly ate her breakfast and left quickly so as not to be late for the bus. She arrived at the university half an hour early. She began to contemplate the place, walking slowly as if she were taking in everything with her eyes, capturing in her heart the scent of the trees, the footsteps of the students, and the sunlight filtering through the campus buildings. The campus had an aura she hadn't experienced in a long time.

Everything was different: the bag on her shoulder, the new notebook in her hands, the smell of coffee, and the racing pulse in her chest. But she didn't look like those young students who walked with the lightness of the present, without a burdened past or a memory filled with anticipation. She carried an entire lifetime on her back, yet she arrived. She arrived, albeit late.

She entered the hall, trembling but walking proudly. Her eyes sparkled as if she were telling the world, "It's not too late. Age hasn't stolen all my dreams from me... I have some left, and now I am living them." She sat in the back seat, even though she longed for the front seat. But something inside her whispered to her to start from the back, to observe first, and to adapt quietly. She was trying not to attract attention.

But she felt all eyes on her. Scattered laughter, hushed whispers, messages flying between the seats, an atmosphere that wasn't entirely foreign.

She'd experienced something similar when she was studying at the institute in Baghdad, but she knew this time was different. This time, she was studying for herself. She silently asked herself:

"Will I master this new world? Will they feel me?" Do I deserve this place?

She lightly grabbed her pen and wrote in the margin of her new notebook: "Age doesn't stand in the way of a dream... but it tests our patience for it." The professor entered the hall, and silence fell. She raised her eyes to him, feeling as if she were once again a child looking at her first teacher. He smiled at her when he noticed her different presence, then said in a clear voice:

"Knowledge knows no age... and the one sitting here today is someone who chose to rise again."

Then he added:

"Please welcome with me your new colleague, Nahla."

Light applause, words of welcome, and kind smiles surrounded her. A smile crept across her lips, and she felt the chair she was sitting on begin to take root in her heart. She repeated to herself:

"When dreams bloom late, their fragrance is deeper... and more fragrant."

When she returned from university in the afternoon, she wasn't feeling tired; she was lighthearted, as if she had just landed on the clouds of a long-awaited dream. She took off her shoes at the door and smiled to herself, then quickly grabbed her phone and called her brother Omar, the person closest to her heart.

"I'm telling you, Omar! Let me tell you what happened today at university... Imagine, the professor welcomed me in front of the students. I felt like I was twenty years old, not fifty."

Omar laughed heartily and encouraged her as usual, leaving a trace of reassurance in her voice that she hadn't found anywhere else. She ended the call, then went into the kitchen and prepared lunch as if she were playing a special tune. Today, she had been cooking with great joy. She ate her food calmly, then sat on the couch to relax a little. Her eyes felt heavy for a moment, but she persevered. She got up, organized her papers and university notebooks. She loves computers, and sat down to review her lessons with determination. As she was reading and reviewing her study materials, the rays of the afternoon sun filtered through the curtains. She walked over and opened her window overlooking the garden. She just wanted to get some fresh air, but she saw something that surprised her.

A gazelle!... It was running lightly and gracefully, heading toward the nearby forest. She quickly got up, grabbed her phone, and tried to take a picture, but the gazelle was faster than her. It disappeared between the trees as if it had emerged from a fleeting dream.

She stood there, laughing to herself, then whispered to herself:

"I won't let anything slip away from me anymore... I will be quick like you, to catch up with what I've missed."

That simple moment was like a message, as if life was whispering to her that hope doesn't run far; it only needs you to run toward it to achieve your dream.

Chapter Sixteen

(1)
Autumn and Winter Carnival

Sometimes, we only discover our strength when it is planted in strange soil and forced to grow.

Three months after starting her university studies, Nahla entered the heart of autumn in Toronto. Autumn there was something different than what she was used to when she lived in Baghdad and the Emirates. The air was saturated with the scent of falling leaves, the sky was sometimes gray, and rain showers competed with the first snowflakes. But it was unexpected; it wasn't overwhelming for her. On the contrary, autumn was the beginning of an inner transformation. She loved the sound of rain falling on the glass windows, and the colors of the fallen leaves were a joy and a delight to the eye. For the first time, Nahla fell in love with autumn for the colors it brings that dazzle the eye and soothe the aching soul. She also loved the coolness that turned hot coffee into a sacred ritual. Even the sprinkles of snow, which she was seeing for the first time, seemed like whispers from a new world beckoning her to discover.

Nahla was at the peak of her energy. Every morning, she would go out wrapped in her protective coat, walking among the wet sidewalks and colorful trees. She loved Canadian autumn because its colorful trees brought joy and happiness to the soul, and her journey to university brought her psychological comfort. She felt something changing within her: her self-confidence, her curiosity to learn more, and even her ambitions.

University life, despite its challenges, gave her a deep sense of belonging and independence.

On weekends, laziness was not an option. She was either at Abu Hilal's store, working while making new connections with customers, or receiving visits from her brothers Omar and Maha, who never let her feel lonely. Her time was filled with assignments and dreams that began to take shape and became a reality. She was no longer just a student at a university in Toronto; she was a girl beginning to redefine herself, learning how to love the seasons she had never known before, and how to make a new beginning out of her exile.

One evening, Nahla was sitting on a wooden bench in the forest near her house. In front of her was a small lake, enjoying the sight of ducks, geese, and squirrels surrounding her as she fed them.

Surrounded by trees that were beginning to lose their leaves one by one, Maha approached her, carrying two cups of tea and said:

"Anyone who sees you now wouldn't believe you were afraid of the cold and alienation."

She took a deep breath and replied:

"I didn't expect autumn to be this warm... not warm in the weather, but warm inside, as if every leaf that falls from a tree makes room for me to start over."

Maha:

"Have you grown to love rain and cold?" Nahla laughed:

"I've loved rain since I was a child, but here I learned to listen to it... The sound of rain on the sidewalk whispers that there is time to accomplish a lot and to explore yourself."

Maha:

"You've become a poet, too." Nahla smiled:

"University changes you, and the cold teaches." I feel like I'm part of a city that's raining dreams, and my dreams, even if they're small, will grow here.

Winter soon began to impose its majesty on Toronto... that unforgiving winter, with its winds that whip faces and temperatures that drop to below thirty degrees below zero. The streets are covered in snow, windows are frosted outside, and the days seem to shrink under the weight of the cold. However, this cold was not enough to stop Nahla. Every morning, she would put on layers of heavy clothes, wrap a scarf around her neck, and go out, stepping over the accumulated snow, heading towards university.

Going to school was not just an obligation; it was her window into herself. Every day, she learned something new from her classmates about them, their customs, and traditions, despite their diverse ethnicities, for Canada is an immigrant society... She was rediscovering herself.

Although most of her classmates were younger than her and of different nationalities, she didn't feel isolated. On the contrary, she felt that she somehow belonged to them, as if experience alone united ages, not years. As for studying, it was another world, with all its fatigue and passion. What attracted her most was the course that taught her how to deal with the elderly, how to understand them, and to feel the pain that they don't express, and how to absorb their anger and heal their tired souls.

With the beginning of this difficult semester, she made the decision to no longer visit Abu Hilal's store often. It wasn't easy; the place made her feel warm and belonging, but it was no longer a priority.

Studying began to become more difficult, turning from a mere challenge into a real test of her strength and ability to balance, but as usual, she did not back down. She knew that the most difficult path was what would make her something new, make her stronger and more mature, so she was ready for what was coming.

(2)
Between Two Years... and Two Cloaks

Sometimes, in the bitter cold, warmth is born from a small dream that resides in the heart... not from the heat of the fireplace

Nahla was approaching the end of her first semester, and at the same time, the last days of 2015 were quietly slipping by. Outside, winter was imposing its stillness, and the cold was wrapping the city like a cloak of frost. But inside Nahla's heart, a strange warmth was pulsing, a warmth resembling a moment of contentment, or the beginning of a dream taking shape.

The winter break arrived after the end of her first semester... two weeks of anticipation and comfort, between the hope of passing her December exams and planning a new trip for the winter semester that begins in January. Despite the cold weather, the days were warm with feelings. Her brother Omar had invited her to visit them and spend unforgettable days.

With his family, it was a wonderful vacation filled with conversations with her mother and siblings, and laughter gathered around a table of love and reassurance.

But something inside her was searching for her own time, something to fill the moments of stillness with passion. In Nahla's heart lay a long-standing love of sewing, a longing for threads that met on a piece of fabric, fashioning a cloak that spoke volumes of her soul.

She told Omar with a dreamy smile, "I want a sewing machine... I want to sew clothes and design cloaks, leaving my mark on them."

Omar didn't hesitate, as if he knew that this gift he was giving her wasn't just a machine, but an extension of her dream. When she returned home to Toronto, Omar took her to a sewing machine store and bought her a sewing machine and accessories. She was overjoyed, and she didn't have to wait long. She sat down, spread out the fabrics, and began cutting and sewing abayas in an authentic Arab style, infusing them with something from the

East and something from her heart. In each piece, she sewed a memory etched in her heart and soul, envisioning a future resembling hers in exile.

On the morning of the first day of 2016, while the holiday atmosphere was still quietly fading from the city's streets and the hearts of its residents, Nahla woke up early, preparing to resume her studies with the start of the second semester.

The winter break had ended, and with it, a new phase had begun. But these were not just ordinary school days. They were a true test, not only of her intelligence, but also of her strength, patience, and self-belief as she embarked on this experience abroad, far from the warmth of her family, with no room for failure or retreat. She knew fully well that there was no room for failure, as her dictionary didn't recognize it.

Everything she had achieved was not a coincidence, but the fruit of long sleepless nights, tiring tears, and an internal struggle during which she wanted to prove to herself, before anyone else, that she was capable. She finished her first semester exams before the end of December, but she emerged from them in a state of anticipation and questioning, as a week of intense anticipation began. Anxiety consumed every detail of her day, tension enveloped every moment, and an incessant inner voice whispered: "Didn't I do my best? Did I do enough?"

In the first week of January, the results appeared. She sat in front of the computer screen, her eyes flicking between the words, eagerly scanning the university website. When the results appeared, she read the word she'd been waiting for: "Pass." But for her, it was more than that. It meant "I made it." She gasped with joy, breathing a sigh of relief for the first time in weeks.

Without hesitation, she immediately picked up the phone and called her mother. When she told her, there was a moment of silence, then her mother's voice burst out in prayer, mixed with tears of joy.

Omar was also happy from the bottom of his heart, as if her success was his own. As for Alaa and Howaida, they were present in her heart as always, even if distance separated them. Their joy was a source of pride and a support to her back. With the end of this tension, the short university break began before the start of the second semester. Two weeks of well-deserved rest, during which she gathered her strength, before returning to her school desks, but this time with greater determination, a more confident heart, and eyes that saw the dream closer than ever.

That night, she went to bed to relax, as if she wanted to remove the fatigue of the past months from her shoulders. She grabbed her pen, opened her notebook, and wrote on the first page of the new year:

"Sometimes, in the depths of winter, warmth is born from a small dream that resides in the heart... not from the heat of the heater."

Chapter Seventeen

(1)
From the Classroom to the Bazaar Corner

The time between seasons... may be the most beautiful season

Nahla began her two-week study break, not as a time for rest, but as an irreplaceable opportunity. She decided to fill every minute with passion and hard work. She would wake up every morning and head to Abu Hilal's shop, working hard and determinedly. In the evening, she would return home, where her small room had become a lively workshop. She would cut and sew abayas with her bare fingers, breathing a bit of her soul into each piece, until each abaya told a story, and each thread narrate a part of her dream. She would not repeat designs, for the creativity in her heart was always renewed, and she always aspired to leave an impact... not to imitate.

One day, while she was working as usual in the shop, a well-known customer came in with a warm smile and invited them to participate in the Arab community bazaar, which is organized by Arab communities during holidays and occasions to preserve what remains of their homelands in the heart of exile. Nahla was excited and approached with shyness mixed with dreaminess, asking to participate by displaying her abayas. Nadia, the exhibition organizer, welcomed her request with joy and told her that she would allocate a corner for her with the Iraqi community, in the middle of an exhibition that included most of the Arab communities.

This was the first exhibition Nahla participated in while living abroad. She entered it with a heart full of hope. As soon as the exhibition ended, her joy was overwhelming. She had sold a number of cloaks and made a small profit, but to her it was as big as a treasure. More beautiful than the profit were the new relationships she formed with women from different Arab communities. Her sense of belonging to this diverse community was indescribable. The warmth in her eyes was the true accomplishment.

Before going to sleep on the last day of her vacation, she took her notebook out of her drawer and wrote:

"In the heart of exile, I discovered that the thread doesn't just connect fabrics... it connects my heart to my dream, my memory... and my roots."

Nahla returned to school at the beginning of the second semester, carrying in her heart a burning passion and unwavering energy. She was fully aware that this semester was heavier than the previous one, as it was full of subjects and studies, but her eyes did not know how to slow down. She chose to move forward strongly, dividing her time between focusing on her studies and working in Abu Hilal's shop. She held on to the details of her day as if she was weaving them like the threads of a cloak.

On weekends, she knew how to gift herself with moments worth cherishing. Sometimes she sits with Maha, sharing lunch or dinner, where conversation warms the heart, especially if it involves passion, loved ones, and mutual friends. Sometimes, she returns to sewing, crafting masterpieces that speak volumes about her taste. A week wouldn't be complete without visiting her brother Omar and his family, where the warmth of family and the salt of nostalgia were present.

She would steal a few hours from her vacation to go to the forest and sit by the lake, where the tranquility and calm of nature reigned, a special place she considered her paradise. There, she would sit and listen to nature's conversation. The sound of gurgling water played a wonderful symphony with the whispering of the trees when the wind caressed them. Her soul was in harmony with them, as if a hidden melody played on the strings of her heart.

At the height of profound harmony between life and responsibility, between striving and serenity, Nahla realized she was no longer lost. She had found herself, standing firmly on the ground upon which she walked with confidence. The dream is no longer far away, nor is the road foggy.

Her steps carried her toward her goal, quietly, and with determination to achieve what she aspired to. In her notebook, she wrote:

"I learned that the heaviest days do not break us if we beat them with willpower, and that in the small corners of life, there hides a comfort that silently repairs the heart."

(2)
Isabel

In some fleeting encounters, blessings are hidden that cannot be seen. True giving is not forgotten, even if it was for a moment.

The second semester was more challenging than the first, but Nahla had set a clear goal for herself: to focus on her studies and sewing. Financial issues didn't worry her much; she had enough to cover housing, food, and other daily obligations.

Therefore, she decided to invest her time in developing her sewing skills, especially designing cloaks, which were admired by a number of women in the community, especially those from the Arab communities. The orders were few, but they filled her heart with satisfaction. Every abaya she sewed carried a piece of her soul. She found in this work an outlet that occupied her free time and generated a small income without interfering with her studies.

For the first time, she felt she was managing her time in a balanced way, combining ambition with dedication.

One day, she finished her classes early and decided to take the opportunity to go to the mall to buy fabric and some sewing supplies. As she was browsing through the rolls of fabric, busy choosing colors and textures, she accidentally bumped into an elderly woman walking slowly. The woman appeared to be in her mid-seventies, with pale features but a calm dignity.

Nahla quickly apologized:

"Sorry, I didn't see you."

The woman smiled gently and said in a low voice: "It's okay, dear."

Nahla noticed that the woman was exhausted, her body barely able to carry her. A humane impulse prompted her to ask without hesitation:

"Can I help you?"

The woman hesitated for a moment, then said calmly: "If you have time... I would be grateful."

Nahla left everything behind and accompanied her to help her choose what she needed. She carried the bags for her and made sure to walk beside her step by step.

In a quiet moment, the woman introduced herself, saying: "I'm Isabel, and I live in a nursing home."

Nahla responded with all kindness:

"I'm Nahla, an Iraqi living here to study."

They chatted on their way to the waiting area, where Isabelle was waiting for a car for people with special needs. Nahla stayed with her until the car arrived and helped her with it.

Before she closed the door, she turned to her and said with genuine kindness:

"Can I call you sometimes? Talking to you has been comforting."

Nahla was overjoyed, and they exchanged phone numbers. Isabelle promised she would call soon. She waved goodbye and then went back to complete her shopping, feeling that something beautiful had just happened. When she arrived home, she sat looking at the fabrics she had bought, but she couldn't ignore the strange feeling that filled her heart. She didn't know if her happiness was due to meeting Isabel, or because she felt she'd been helpful and had offered something simple but sincere!

It was a quiet, different joy, one that came from a deep place... from a genuine human touch on a day she hadn't expected anything from. When the time came for bed, she couldn't sleep at first, and something remained in her mind.

It was a strange feeling she couldn't explain. But as usual, she opened her notebook to document the day's events, writing:

"Sometimes, life doesn't give us joy from the things we seek, but from a simple human moment we didn't plan for."

A few days later, Nahla's phone suddenly rang. Nahla answered quickly, and a name appeared on the screen that she hadn't memorized before, but it sounded familiar. As soon as she answered, she heard a calm, warm voice on the other end.

"Hello, Nahla, I'm Isabel... the lady you met at the mall." Happiness flooded Nahla's voice as she greeted her warmly, as if she had been anticipating this call from deep within, without realizing it. They exchanged conversation for a few minutes that seemed shorter than she had hoped. During that time, Isabel invited her to visit her at the nursing home where she lived. She didn't hesitate, but enthusiastically agreed. She felt something akin to nostalgia. Although this relationship was still in its infancy, there was a special warmth about it, as if this invitation might be the beginning of something bigger that she hadn't yet realized.

They agreed on Saturday, the weekend, and Isabelle gently insisted that Nahla spend the entire day with her. Unable to refuse this friendly insistence, she smiled and said, "I'll be with you in the morning."

On the appointed day, Nahla woke up early, thinking of something special to do for this visit. An idea occurred to her:

"Why don't I cook her something from my country?"

She headed to the kitchen and began preparing dolma, one of the most famous and distinctive Iraqi dishes. She poured her heart into the cooking, carefully choosing the vegetables, and seasoning the filling with a traditional spirit that carried the scent of her homeland. She wondered, would she like it? Would she accept a different culture? Would the nursing home, as they say, be a formal, cold, and restrictive place?

But when she arrived at the nursing home, all those questions faded and were replaced by amazement. The place resembled a spacious, warm house, with a large, elegant garden in front and a reception hall decorated with pictures and drawings, vibrant with life, not isolation. The facilities were clean and tidy, and the staff smiled warmly, as if they knew visitors by name.

Isabel greeted her at the door. She was wearing a light blue wool jacket, the color of the sky, and black pants. She had a yellow shawl mixed with blue over her shoulders, and her face beamed with joy.

She spontaneously extended her arms and said, "How happy I am. Because you came."

She took her on a tour of the home and talked to her about the place. She said with a proud smile:

"This place isn't government-owned. We pay a monthly fee to stay here, so we have more freedom to host visitors and stay with them as we please.

Free homes have their own rules, but private homes have their own rules."

Nahla was amazed. She hadn't expected to find this level of dignity and privacy in a nursing home. After the tour, they entered Isabelle's small room. It was tastefully arranged, with personal touches: pictures of colorful flower books in a glass vase, and a curtain with spring patterns.

They sat together. Nahla opened the food bowl and gently placed the plate in front of her. She said:

"This dish is called 'dolma,' and it's a traditional Iraqi dish. I wanted you to taste something from my country."

Isabelle took a small bite, then paused, looked at Nahla with genuine surprise, and said excitedly:

"This is the first time I've tasted food with such a wonderful flavor. It's amazing. What are all these spices that have a unique taste I've never tasted before?"

Nahla laughed and began to explain to her the ingredients of the dish: stuffed vegetables with rice, meat, and lemon flavor, and how dolma brings the whole family together at one table.

Isabel seemed to enjoy not only the food, but also the story Nahla was telling. She then asked several questions about Iraq, holidays and occasions, childhood, food, and memories.

Nahla said with a smile:

"Next time, I'll bring you another dish. We have many foods with distinctive, unforgettable flavors."

Isabel replied:

"And I'll look forward to it, Nahla. Your presence here today has brought me happiness I haven't felt in a long time."

At that moment, Nahla felt something deep stir in her heart. It wasn't just a visit or a plate of food; it was the beginning of a wonderful relationship that transcended language, age, and culture. It was a small coincidence that turned into a true human bond that could transform her loneliness and give her alienation a new flavor.

After they finished lunch, Isabelle suggested to her guest that they move to the large living room for tea. She agreed with a grateful smile, but inside, she felt curiosity like the rustling of leaves in a light wind. Many questions swirled in her mind about this place, which surprised her with its level of luxury and refined care.

As they sat quietly in a corner overlooking the back garden, Nahla turned to Isabel hesitantly but sincerely and said:

"Let me ask you about this house. Honestly, I was surprised by its construction. It's like a five-star hotel. Everything here exudes care, from the gym to the TV room to the private dining room. I noticed that you have a great deal of freedom, as you can dine in your rooms if you wish. Are all these services free, or are they subject to a charge?"

Isabel laughed gently, as if she had been anticipating this question from the first moment, and said:

"I understand your curiosity, and it's perfectly justified. The truth is, I decided to move to this place after loneliness started to eat away at the edges of my days. My children grew up, got married, and each went his own way. I was living in a very large house, but its emptiness screamed at me every night. I couldn't stand the loneliness, so I decided to rent the house and come here. Yes, I pay a considerable amount of money monthly, but what I get in return is priceless. Comfort, care, and most importantly... I don't eat my breakfast in silence; there is someone to share it with."

Nahla felt embarrassed and bowed slightly, apologizing:

"I hope I didn't overstep my bounds. I didn't mean to interfere in your private affairs."

Isabel smiled warmly and extended her hand gently toward Nahla's, saying:

"Don't apologize. I'm the one who thanks you. Sometimes, speaking about what's in your heart lightens the burden. Loneliness isn't like the isolation we choose; it's like a gray cloud that blocks the light and weighs down the air. Here, at least, I find someone to share time and conversation with, and I feel like I'm not living on the margins of life."

Nahla shook her head, moved, as if the elderly woman's words had opened a window into a new face of life in Canada, one that, behind meticulous care, concealed souls seeking warmth, not just services. Sipping her tea slowly, Isabel said:

"You've made me eager to hear more about your country."

Nahla raised her head as if she were removing the veil of time and said in a tone that blended pride and nostalgia:

"If I talk to you about Iraq, I am talking to you about the heart of history, about a land that wrote the first letters and planted the first seeds.

Iraq is not just a homeland; it is the memory of humanity and the cradle of civilizations. The civilizations of Mesopotamia—Babylon, Assyria, and Sumer—all wrote the greatest stories on the banks of the two great rivers, the Tigris and Euphrates. As for Baghdad, it is a poem still sung with the most wonderful melodies, a bride wearing the cloak of One Thousand and One Nights. As for my city, Adhamiyah, overlooking the Tigris River from the Rusafa direction, it is not just love, but a story that pulsates in my heart.

Every alleyway tells a story, and every scent takes me back to my childhood, to the bread baked in the oven, to its markets, and to the neighbors who are closer to us than family."

Isabel's eyes followed Nahla with amazement and interest, as if her words were painting a real scene before her. After a moment of silence, Isabel whispered:

"Tomorrow is Sunday... Can I ask for a small favor?" Nahla raised her eyebrows in surprise:

"Of course, say what you want."

Isabel said, a secret gleam in her eyes:

"I'd really like you to visit me again. I have so much to talk to you about, and I want to make a suggestion that might change your life."

Nahla's eyes widened in surprise, and she asked curiously: "And what is this suggestion?"

Isabel laughed lightly and said:

"I'll tell you tomorrow, at tea time."

Then she bid farewell to Nahla with warm words and left her hoping to meet again tomorrow. When Nahla returned to her residence, she was not as she had left. Her steps were normal, but deep down there was something new moving. It was as if her heart was knocking on a door that hadn't been opened for a long time... a door behind which stood a surprise, or perhaps a new life waiting to write its first lines.

Chapter Eighteen

(1)
Dialogue with the Roots

Sometimes, being away from family is not a rupture, but a quiet way to protect what remains of love

Nahla returned to her apartment after visiting Isabel. It was four in the afternoon. She lay on her bed, a strange feeling coming over her. She felt comfortable, but there was something missing, as if any joy she experienced was always incomplete. While she was relaxing, it occurred to her to call her mother, as it was now ten in the evening in Abu Dhabi. She opened her phone and made a video call via WhatsApp.

Her mother answered, and to her surprise, all her brothers and sisters were gathered at home. Joy spread across her mother's face as soon as she saw her, and her brothers began talking and joining in the conversation, asking about her status.

Jumana interrupted the conversation by asking:

"Nahla, have you found a job? How do you spend your time? What do you do?"

Nahla laughed, understanding the meaning behind Jumana's question, then answered with a smile:

"I currently work temporarily in an Arab shop, and I'm still looking for a permanent job."

Here, Ayad interjected with his usual question, full of veiled sarcasm: "Do you work as a maid or a saleswoman?"

His sarcastic tone was clear, as Nahla was accustomed to his bullying and provocations, which often made her nervous, especially his famous phrase:

"You don't know anything and you don't understand." Which he repeats constantly, sometimes accompanied by calling her stupid. But this time, Nahla decided to respond in a different way. She was uncharacteristically calm and said:

"My dear, here in Canada, there is no luxury like Abu Dhabi. Everyone is humble and doesn't compare themselves to the Asian worker. Everyone here is equal. The shop I work in is an Arab shop, and I've learned a lot from it and gained good experience. Most importantly, people don't depend on their brothers financially, and they don't emotionally blackmail them in the name of brotherhood."

Ayad did not complete the conversation with her and said goodbye to her quickly and at the same time.

Jumana could respond to her, especially after Nahla's response to Ayad was very clear. Jumana knew that if she went too far and said words that Nahla didn't like, she would hear things that she didn't like. Nadine broke the conversation to ease the tension that had begun, saying in a surprised tone:

"Are you comfortable? Why all this suffering? Come back and I will allocate you a monthly salary."

Nahla felt the need to control her nerves and responded calmly:

"Nadine, when you visited us, you gave me $100 as a gift and said that was enough for me. When I took you shopping, you only shopped for Marwan, his children and his wife, and also for Jumana's children. But if I wanted to buy something for myself, you said: "I gave you your gift."

Nadine was surprised by Nahla's response and seemed more nervous than Jumana, so she replied:

"So you were keeping all of this inside your heart?" Nahla responded calmly:

"Yes, and this is the most important reason that makes me free in every sense of the word. Thank you very much for everything you have done for me. Thanks to you all, I am now a new Nahla."

Before the tension could escalate, their mother intervened to ask gently: "Are you eating well, my daughter?"

Nahla smiled and responded tenderly:

"Praise be to God, Mom, I'm in perfect health and well-being. God willing, God will decree good things for me according to my intentions."

Nahla felt the tension rising in the family because of her conversation, so she decided to politely end the call and bid them farewell with a warm smile and warm kisses. When she hung up, she noticed something had changed inside her. For the first time, she didn't cry out of sadness or longing for her family. Instead, she realized that separation is sometimes better for preserving love.

An hour had passed since Nahla ended her call with her family, but the painful memories refused to leave her in peace. She was trying to occupy herself with preparing lunch for the next day, and chose to cook "Tamen Baqala," rice with green broad beans and dill, accompanied by oven- roasted chicken. As she was chopping the dill, the memory of Nadine crept into her mind, as if she didn't want to forget it, as if she had been waiting for a moment like this to return with all its pain.

Nadine had always been the most mysterious and cruel of the family. Every time Nahla tried to bury the past, it would creep back through the cracks of her memory. She remembered Nadine's visits when she was first married, and how she treated her with cold arrogance, as if she weren't her sister, but rather a less important being. Nahla felt invisible, and that her love wasn't reciprocated. Nahla grew older, and with her those wounds grew.

When Nadine separated from her first husband and returned to the family home, she wasn't the same. Rather, she acted as if she were stuck in a spiral of anger and silence. At that time, Nahla was looking for a job after graduating from the Institute of Management, while Nadine transferred her job to Baghdad.

Despite living with the family, the distance between them grew wider and wider.

She bitterly remembered how Nadine avoided her and avoided speaking to her. She wouldn't even speak to her. Her words were few and stingy, and her language was those looks that were not devoid of contempt and bullying, especially when Jumana was around when she visited the family. She wasn't the sister she'd dreamed of being a supporter, but rather a stranger, living with a family she didn't know, as if she were forced to

Then came the anniversary of Nadine's engagement to her second husband, and the day she decided to receive the groom's family at her aunt's house, far from the family home. It was as if she wanted to erase her connection to them. After the marriage, she traveled to Norway, leaving behind a scar in the hearts of her family, especially Nahla, that never healed. On every visit, Nadine treated Nahla in a hurtful manner. She would smile and hug her on the first day with longing, then return to her usual coldness after two days or more. She would give her a small amount of money but she always reminded her that she did it out of generosity. '

She was asking to go shopping with her, buying for everyone, and when Nahla asked for something simple, the usual phrase came: "I gave you a hundred dollars, and that's enough for you."

Nahla turned to her mother crying, complaining about the harsh treatment she received from her sister, but her mother always said:

"Be patient, she is our guest."

Nahla didn't know if this patience meant love or remain silent about injustice. All of this made her wonder to herself, in a voice no one could hear:

"Why do they treat me so harshly? What have I done to them? Why don't they love me as much as they love Marwan and Jumana? Why do they give them everything and leave me to watch? Am I a burden to them or a mistake in the family arrangement?"

She sighed, but she felt that this time the sigh wasn't as heavy as before. It was as if something inside her was starting to breathe freely. She returned to the kitchen, a slight smile on her face, as if she was trying to create a light moment for herself amidst all this heaviness. She muttered lightly as she stirred the pot of rice:

"I wonder... what Isabel will surprise me with tomorrow?"

With her evening cup of coffee, she had her usual evening of finishing schoolwork. In a moment, she took out her notebook and wrote:

"Some wounds don't bleed; however they steal your warmth whenever memory smiles."

(2)
Drops of Dream

When you walk your path with faith and honesty, you will find that kind hands extend to you from where you do not expect, as if fate is rewarding you for your hidden patience

Nahla woke up on Sunday morning to a soft chill enveloping the city, and the sky covered with heavy clouds as if whispering the promise of rain.

The temperature was around 2 degrees Celsius, but her warmth overcame the chill. She got out of bed with quiet energy and looked at her watch; it was 6:30 in the morning. Without hesitation, she put on her warm coat, prepared a cheese sandwich and a cup of tea with milk, and then walked toward the forest behind her house. Despite the cold weather and the heavy sky, she felt she needed a moment of contemplation near the lake, as she did every week, gathering her strength and reorganizing the chapters of her heart.

Visits to the forest became an indispensable ritual. The trees swayed as if they knew her, and deer and squirrels appeared from time to time, as if to greet her with familiarity. The sounds of birdsong, the gurgling of water, and the wind caressing her face all played an unwritten, yet lived, symphony.

Each time she visited this place, she felt as if nature had presented her with a new canvas of beauty, one she had never seen before.

She sat on the wooden bench by the lake, eating her breakfast in grateful silence. Suddenly, she saw a group of ducks approaching her across the surface of the water. She laughed softly and broke her sandwich to them, as if sharing a breakfast with them that carried the flavor of reassurance. Moments later, the rain began to fall gently. Its drops were light and refreshing, as if it were cleansing the soul before the earth. Instead of rushing home, she decided to continue walking under it, inhaling the air, and letting every drop that touched her face be a love letter from heaven. She walked with certainty in her heart: no matter how uncertain tomorrow might be, she would continue striving to make her dream come true.

When she returned home, it wasn't the end of her day; it was just beginning.

She got ready again, carrying lunch on her way to visit her dear friend, Isabel, the woman who had become like a second family to her while abroad. At half past twelve in the afternoon, her new friend was sitting in the lounge of the nursing home waiting for her. She had prepared to meet her since the morning, even though she knew that lunch would be at one o'clock. When the clock struck the exact time, Nahla entered, smiling, carrying boxes of food and the scent of love.

Isabel said, smiling:

"Good evening, Nahla! I was waiting for you impatiently. I prepared since morning even though I knew you would come at noon"

Nahla hugged her gently and replied:

"Good evening, Isabelle. I'm sorry if I kept you waiting. But our appointment was for lunch."

The lady laughed, saying:

"Don't apologize, I know that, but my longing for you and for the Iraqi lunch made the wait long. Lunch has a different taste when I eat it with you."

They smiled together, then Isabel invited her to share a cup of coffee in the living room before they ate. They sat in a comfortable and friendly atmosphere, exchanging glances and simple words that carried a lot of unconditional love. After a few moments of comfortable silence, Isabelle asked a question from a loving heart:

"Excuse me, my friend, I don't like to intrude on your privacy, but since our first meeting, I've felt that you're like my younger sister, or perhaps my eldest daughter. How long have you been here in Canada?"

Nahla answered without hesitation, with frankness that exuded confidence:

"No need to apologize, dear Isabel. Ask whatever you want. I came to Canada last year on a two-year study visa. I'm now studying at the University of Toronto for a two-year diploma in "Healthcare and Life

Sciences." I also work for daily wages in an Arab shop, and I also design and sew abayas. I even participated in an exhibition for the Arab community a short while ago."

Isabel raised her eyebrows in surprise mixed with admiration and said:

"So you're looking for a permanent job... and what else are you good at?" Nahla smiled humbly and replied:

"As I told you, I'm a skilled seamstress, and even a fashion designer for children and teenagers, as well as traditional abayas. I have experience working with the elderly and people with special needs."

Isabel laughed gently and said:

"And you're also a great cook. I can't forget your delicious food." They laughed together, and Nahla said enthusiastically:

"I hope to find a job opportunity here, and I promise that I will cook you an Iraqi dish every day."

Isabel held her hand and said sincerely:

"I am confident that you will succeed, and I promise that I will help you achieve your dreams."

Nahla said with great emotion:

"You are wonderful, Isabel. I feel that God answered my prayers when I arrived in Canada. I was asking Him to take care of my affairs, and now you are helping me."

Isabel smiled and said gently:

"Don't thank me. I am the one who should thank you for this meeting. I have many friends who have power and influence here in

Toronto. Give me your papers and resume, and I will do my best to present them to them.

Who knows, maybe this will be the beginning of your new life."

Nahla couldn't believe what she was hearing. Her eyes welled up with emotion, and she held Isabel's hand tightly, saying:

"You are more than I have dreamed of. May God bless you and give you all the best."

Isabel replied with a warm smile:

"This is just the beginning, Nahla... The future is before you, and I am here to help you every step of this long way and will not leave you."

It's lunch time. Nahla approached Isabelle with a warm smile and whispered gently:

"Would you please show me the way to the kitchen, or accompany me so we can set the table together?"

Isabel nodded in agreement, a welcoming sparkle in her eyes, and then led her into the kitchen, where the beautiful scents began their journey. It wasn't an hour until the kitchen was transformed into a world of joy, and the dining table was filled with the colors of dishes and their delicious aromas. Isabelle looked at the table, her eyes wide with amazement:

"Wow! What is this? It's a feast."

Nahla laughed lightly, then began to lovingly list the details of the dishes:

"This is green rice, or as we say in Iraq, "temman baqala." Rice mixed with green beans and dill, a distinctive dish on our Iraqi table. As for this, it is chicken roasted in the oven, "tabsi" style, with potatoes, onions, and garlic, drenched in a spiced sauce and olive oil."

Then she pointed to a side dish:

"And here's a light salad of fresh vegetables, flavored with oregano.

Rest assured, the food is healthy, as we've all started to be careful about cholesterol."

They sat down to lunch in an atmosphere of intimacy and pleasure, and every bite carried with it flavor and emotion. As the minutes passed, Isabel put down her fork, looked at Nahla with grateful eyes, and said:

"Nahla, you have honored me with indescribable generosity, and fed me from your soul before your food. I would like to return the favor. But honestly, I cannot prepare such wonderful food myself."

She paused for a moment, then continued in a serious tone mixed with tenderness:

"I would like you to do me a favor. Cook me Iraqi food every weekend. I will gladly pay you for it. If you refuse, I will understand, but please don't insist on it for free, as I will not accept it."

Nahla was silent for a moment, overwhelmed with a warm feeling of gratitude for this pure appreciation. Then she smiled and said:

"Thanks, Isabel. I'd be very happy to cook for you this weekend. But let's make a deal."

She raised her eyes to her and added gently:

"I am your guest every time, without obligation or compensation. Let's leave room for generosity to breathe, just like food. Then, I probably won't be able to visit you every weekend because I'm busy studying and sewing, so contact between us will be ongoing."

Isabel laughed heartily and replied:

"Agreed, then."

And between the laughter and life's conversations, lunch wasn't just a meal. It was the beginning of a friendship woven with vegetables and dill, and made with affection and respect.

Chapter Nineteen

(1)
Spring of the Heart

In exile, I did not search for a homeland, but rather created it with my own hands I planted a seed in every challenge, until chapters bloomed within me that the calendar does not know

The days were passing by as if time had rushed them, and the second semester of her first year at university was drawing to a close. Nahla, who had arrived in this country laden with questions and anxiety, was now one of those who knew how to juggle challenges. Between studying, working at Abu Hilal's boutique, and designing abayas, which had become a small business, there was no time to catch her breath.

One morning, she was sitting on her small balcony, sipping her coffee while looking at the trees that had begun to wear the colors of spring. She said to herself in a low voice, as if whispering to herself, "I never imagined that I would endure like this, and even blossom."

Not everything was easy, but she learned that patience is not just waiting, but also hard work and effort. The wonderful thing is that fate did not deny her companionship. She joined a group of Arab immigrant women, each carrying a story of exile, worries, passion, and struggle in the diaspora. They held a bazaar in the heart of Toronto, displaying ceramic artifacts, hand- embroidered items, and abayas with traditional touches. Nahla explained to visitors the story behind each piece she handmade, as if telling a chapter from One Thousand and One Nights.

The exam days passed like a cold storm. The exams were difficult; she couldn't deny that, but the most difficult thing was the fear of failure.

When the results came out, she sat staring at them for a long time: good, acceptable. The grades may not have been brilliant, but they were enough to light up an overwhelming sense of pride inside her. At that moment, she couldn't control herself; she grabbed her phone and called her mother.

The mother burst into tears on the other end, and prayers poured in:

"May God raise your head, my daughter. You've worked hard, and God has compensated you."

Minutes didn't pass before another call came from Omar, her brother, saying:

"Congratulations, family heroine."

She laughed lightly, and a beautiful conversation took place between them: "I swear, Omar, I felt that I would succeed, but I was terrified."

Omar:

"I will come and pick you up. You will spend the summer with us at home. I miss you."

Nahla:

"If possible, Omar, in a week? I have orders for abayas that I must complete. I promised to deliver them to them within the next few days."

Omar:

"So, you are determined to sew, so rest during the vacation and complete your activities at the beginning of the new school year.:

Nahla:

"Omar, I just discovered myself, and honestly, I've started racing against time to reach my goal. In the new school year, I need to find a volunteer position for practical training, and at the same time, I must secure a job now to ensure a hassle-free residency transfer."

Omar:

"I agree with you, and you are free to choose the appropriate time to visit us, and I will help you find a suitable job for you, but do not forget that we miss you, and the children wish to spend time with their aunt."

Nahla ended her call with her brother Omar affectionately. She then phoned her friend Maha, and they decided to go out together to the mall to celebrate her success. That was it. As she strolled down Yonge Street with her friend, carrying fabric bags and sewing supplies, and gazing at shop windows, she smiled to herself and said:

"Strangers have become less strange, and the streets have become familiar. Here in the heart of Toronto, I found myself."

The sky was raining lightly, but they didn't run away. They took their time, their smiling faces telling a distinct success story. Nahla raised her face towards the clouds and said in a low voice that Maha heard:

"This is Canada's spring... and my spring, let us blossom together."

A month after summer vacation, on a sunny morning with rays of light streaming into the living room, she sat with Maha in her house, eating breakfast and chatting about friends. Suddenly, Nahla's phone rang, breaking the silence. She looked at the screen and smiled, saying:

"Isabel."

After exchanging greetings, Isabel's voice came full of enthusiasm, saying:

"Nahla, I have wonderful news for you. I have found you an excellent job opportunity.

Tomorrow, at nine o'clock in the morning, go to the Kaliquay Ready-Made Garments Factory. Bring all your papers with you, and if you have samples or pictures of the clothes you designed, take them too. You will meet Mr.

Jan, the factory manager, and I am confident that you will find your opportunity there."

Nahla was silent for a few seconds, as if she couldn't believe what she'd heard. Then tears of joy streamed down her face. She thanked Isabel warmly and promised to tell her all the details of the interview. As she was hanging up, Maha hugged her tightly and said, smiling:

"I'm so happy for you. Don't worry, I'll take you to the factory tomorrow. Give me the address."

Nahla answered enthusiastically:

"The factory is called Kalikuai Ready-Made Garments Manufacturing, and it's located in Toronto."

Maha quickly searched for the location on Google, and soon the factory details appeared. It was a facility specializing in the production of ready- made garments at affordable prices, serving retailers and small brand owners. It was located only 30 minutes from Nahla's house.

An hour later, Nahla left her friend's house and returned to her own residence, a mixture of excitement and trepidation in her heart.

She began preparing her old designs, reviewing her files, and thinking about the next day. As she was getting ready for bed early, a question suddenly weighed heavily on her heart:

"If I work at the factory in the evening and study at university in the morning, when will I find time for the volunteer work I've planned? How will I reconcile my studies in healthcare, my passion for sewing, and my other commitments? Won't that be too much for me?"

Because she didn't like making crucial decisions while she was confused, she decided to call her brother Omar, who had always been the voice of reason in her life. Omar answered in his calm voice:

"Nahla, my dear, you're at a crossroads now. You can either continue your studies in healthcare and life sciences or pursue a career in sewing.

Sewing is beautiful, and you're talented at it, but you should focus on your specialization, especially since you'll soon start volunteer work. It's best to find an opportunity that aligns with your studies."

Omar's words were sweet. She knew deep down that he was right. Rushing into the garment factory might not help her in the long run. The next morning, she called Isabel, her heart heavy with confusion.

She spoke frankly about her struggle between passion and future. Isabel responded tenderly:

"You're right. Your time is limited, and your effort is spread across many tasks. I believe you should focus on what benefits your professional future. As for sewing, it will stay a hobby or side project when the time comes, and the work at Abu Hilal's store will stay the same."

Nahla felt a deep sense of relief, despite her sadness at having to postpone her dream of sewing.

She thanked Isabel, saying:

"I'm sorry I bothered you. I won't go to the interview." Isabel replied, laughing:

"It's okay, my dear. I'll wait for you this weekend with your new Iraqi cuisine."

Nahla laughed and said goodbye, hoping to see her soon. More than two weeks passed, and she returned to her usual visits to Isabel. There, her friend surprised her with new news:

"Nahla, I have got approval from the director of the nursing Center to start working as a volunteer caring for the elderly here. With time, you will gain experience, and at the end of the year, you might find a permanent job.

What do you think?"

Nahla's heart nearly leapt with joy. She didn't hesitate and answered confidently:

"I agree without hesitation."

And so, Nahla found the balance she was seeking: She would keep her part-time job with Abu Hilal, dedicate time to sewing to support her bank, and focus on her studies and volunteer work in her field... Finally, she felt that she was walking a path that truly reflected her, one that didn't exhaust her but instead fulfilled her dream step by step. At the end of the road, she realized that maturity doesn't mean giving up on dreams but knowing the right time to pursue them and having the ability to steadily move toward what is worthwhile.

(2)
When She Chose the Path

Sometimes we don't need new paths, but the courage to decide on the path that resembles us

The new academic year began, and with it, a new chapter in Nahla's life. She returned to university with a different feeling.

This time, she wasn't just a student searching for her path. Instead, she felt like a young woman in her twenties who had experienced hesitation and confusion, but then stood up to consciously choose her path with a more mature and confident outlook. She took her first steps into the field of healthcare and life sciences. It marked the peak of her balance between studying, working part-time at Abu Hilal's shop, and volunteering at the elderly care center.

On the first day of school, she carried her bag, carefully placed her books, then looked in the mirror and smiled. Her eyes held a sense of hope and confidence.

She arrived at the university and met her classmates, both male and female. She shook hands with them warmly. They talked about their summer vacation, their worries about this year's classes, and their hopes for the new year. She listened with a smile, but inside she felt she was one step ahead. She had moved past searching for herself and was now building her future.

In the evening, after school, Nahla went to the elderly care center, where she had the chance to volunteer for eight hours a week, spread over several days. There, the residents greeted her with friendly faces and warm smiles.

She began to feel a strange sense of harmony and psychological comfort she had never experienced before, perhaps because she was actually practicing her profession or because she found a special meaning in serving others that went beyond simply earning certificates. During one of the sessions, while helping an elderly woman stand and walk, she felt something take over her heart. There was a brief moment of silence, during which she said to herself:

"This is the place I've been searching for. This is the true meaning of humanity."

The days went by quickly as they filled with school, designing abayas in her spare time, participating in exhibitions to sell them, working at the care center, and putting in hours at Abu Hilal's.

Her days were busy, sometimes exhausting, but they brought her a sense of contentment. Nahla wasn't seeking comfort, but rather a path that showed who she was, and she walked it confidently.

One day, she received an email from the university administration informing her that she was eligible to finish her third year and earn a certificate of excellence. She was surprised and had to make a quick decision, which wasn't easy. She saw it as a golden opportunity that could change her future. She asked for some time to think it over, then quickly called her brother Omar, who had always supported her decisions. She said to him in a voice filled with hesitation:

"Omar, I really need your opinion."

He listened to her patiently, then replied:

Sister, first of all, don't worry about the financial part. I am happy to cover the costs of the excellence year. Second, this year is important not only for academics but also because it completes the time needed to get permanent residency or even citizenship. After you finish your third year, we can change your residency from studying to working, and at the same time, you can earn a more advanced certificate. But you need to decide quickly to avoid fines or getting stuck with incomplete paperwork.

Nahla listened carefully, then paused for a moment, then said clearly:

"But Omar, I'm really enjoying my volunteer work now at a nursing home. The manager said he'd hire me after graduation. I've gotten to know the people here, I love the city, I've adapted to life, and honestly, I feel like this is my place."

She hesitated for a moment, then continued:

Honestly, I want to start a new life without the obligation of studying. I want to work and focus on designing abayas. I feel like I've discovered myself.

Omar smiled and said to her proudly:

"I respect your decision, and I'm with you. You've really started to make your own path steadily. What's important is that you know what you want."

Nahla ended the call and sat on the edge of her bed, looking out the window at the garden she'd become a part of, almost as if she were a part of it. She remembered the first moments she'd arrived, her anxiety gripping her and her thoughts distracted... Then she smiled as she reminisced about her journey and how she'd been able to choose and decide. She opened her notebook and wrote in it:

"This will not be the end of the road, but the beginning of a new life... a life I made with my own hands, with threads of dream and reality, between design and care, between heart and mind."

Nahla completed her second year of study with distinction, receiving a "very good" grade. That grade wasn't just a number on a piece of paper; it was a testament to her hard work and perseverance, and the embodiment of a true journey of maturity. At the elderly care center, she didn't just volunteer, but proved herself worthy with her skills and compassion, until the long-awaited day came when she was officially appointed to the home. The moment she received her work contract was like a fruit that ripened in its time. Tears of joy filled her eyes, and she remembered every moment of doubt and every moment of confusion she had experienced, and she became certain that self-belief and conscious choice open doors she had never seen before.

She whispered to herself as she signed her first job contract. "Today... I officially took the first step in the life I'd long dreamed of."

From university to the elderly care center, Nahla began her career journey. Her first decision was to stop working at the Abu Hilal store to devote all her time to the center, along with her beloved passion: sewing and designing abayas. Her business gradually expanded, and she participated in exhibitions outside her province, and her name began to be known as a designer specializing in abayas, an achievement she had never imagined. But amidst this success, there was a void that no one could fill. Her heart was missing one thing: her mother.

Nostalgia was different for her. She missed her mother's embrace, her siblings' voices, the warmth of her first home. She couldn't travel because of the legal deadline required to submit her paperwork to the Canadian

Citizenship and Citizenship Department. Every call with her mother ended in tears. She felt as if the year was dragging on her heart like a mountain.

After a long year, she finally submitted her paperwork for citizenship. The six months passed painfully slowly until the answer came: her application had been accepted, and she had received a citizenship number. Her joy was indescribable; she could now take an official leave and travel on her first annual vacation.

One summer morning, which coincided with a weekend, she woke up at dawn, ate breakfast, and went to the forest near her house, where she usually sat on her wooden bench. She took out her phone and called her brother Omar:

"Omar, I want to visit my mother and brothers. I've been dreaming about them for a while and I wake up startled. I miss them so much. What do you think about going to Abu Dhabi for two weeks? I want to surprise them."

Omar laughed and said excitedly:

"Great idea! But... do you have any vacation left?" Nahla:

"Yes, I have three whole weeks." Omar:

"Great. I'll arrange the visa for you, and we'll set the travel date soon."

She quickly interrupted him:

"Omar, I can't travel without you. And you haven't seen my mother for a year. Try to take a vacation, even if it's just for ten days. We prepare a nice surprise together."

He hesitated a little, then said:

"Okay, I'll try."

A week later, he called her again, and in a joyful voice: "Good news, I got you a visa... When are we traveling?" She replied without hesitation:

"I'm ready, as soon as possible. Let's book now."

She hung up, her heart pounding like a child waiting for a holiday. She wasn't just due to travel, but for a long-awaited hug, and a tear that would only dry on her mother's shoulder.

A week later, Omar called her to tell her that he had made a reservation for them and that in ten days they would be in their mother's arms.

Chapter Twenty

(1)
The Bird Flies to Visit Loved Ones

In exile, we grow old quickly, but we wither slowly There is no homeland that contains us like a mother's voice on the telephone, nor an embrace that restores us like a step that takes us back to the threshold of the old home

Ten days passed as if slowly, and here we are, Nahla and her brother Omar, flying in the sky, returning to their mother's embrace. On their way to the airport, Omar's phone rang, and it was their mother calling. He said to her: "I'll be near you in a few hours, Mom."

She asked him:

"And what about Nahla?" He answered in a low voice:

"She has circumstances that prevent her from traveling, and God willing, she will visit you soon."

His mother didn't respond, but her heart sank. She'd longed to see her daughter, dreaming of the moment they'd meet for months. On the plane, Nahla looked at Omar sitting next to her and asked:

"Omar, can you invite my mother to visit? I want her with me. If possible, I'll rent an apartment for both of us."

He answered calmly:

"Nahla, inviting her is too easy, but the problem is my mother. You know her well. She can't stand being away from home. She loves our Eastern atmosphere, her home, her neighbors, and the warmth of her family. How will she leave all that to live here?"

His words made sense, but she didn't give in to that small voice inside her, which kept whispering:

"There's no harm in trying... maybe she'll agree." She said firmly:

"We won't lose anything if we try to convince her to visit. It's true that she's in her late seventies, but I feel she'd be delighted if she came, even for a few weeks."

Omar smiled and promised her that he would tell his mother, even though he was certain she would refuse, but trying wouldn't hurt. When the plane arrived at Abu Dhabi Airport in the evening, Ayad was waiting for them. The meeting was full of surprises.

Hugs, kisses, and tears are feelings that cannot be translated into words. Ayad was surprised to find Nahla with Omar. As soon as they got into the car, Ayad called their mother. When their mother heard Nahla's voice on the phone, she burst into tears of joy, as if her heart couldn't believe that it was finally hearing her daughter.

At the door of the house, Adhraa and her mother were waiting for her. The meeting was a storm of hugs, tears of longing, and laughter of nostalgia. In an instant, everything returned to the way it was, as if Nahla had not been away from home for more than three years. The loved ones gathered at the dinner table. Nahla kept looking around, scrutinizing the dining room, the balcony overlooking the sea, and whispering:

"O my God, it's as if I left it yesterday." Adhraa replied with a warm smile:

"And what do you expect? Nothing has changed in this house." Ayad added:

"My mother refuses to let us change anything about it. She likes it to stay the same."

Nahla laughed:

"The most beautiful thing about him is that his mother's touch remains, and the Virgin's blessing shades him. May God perpetuate our love and never separate us."

After dinner, they gathered in the living room to drink tea. Adhraa said gently:

"If you're tired, go rest. Your room is now the guest room." Nahla smiled lovingly and said:

"It's nice that I still have a place in the house, even if the name of my room has changed."

Omar commented jokingly:

"And I'm always the wronged one in the family... There isn't even a bed named after me. Either I share Mom's room or I sleep in the living room."

Everyone laughed. Then each went to their own room, their hearts filled with immeasurable warmth and unbought reassurance. Nahla couldn't sleep because of the time difference, and her unwillingness to waste a single hour without her mother's company kept her awake. She got out of bed before everyone else and prepared breakfast for the family. She didn't feel tired from the journey; it was as if she had never left the house. She was surprised when she learned that Ayad had gone out early in the morning to bring them cream and coffee. She was very happy and added them to the breakfast table.

After that, she went to wake up her mother and Adhraa, as it was the weekend and no one had work commitments. When she entered her mother's room, she found her awake. She kissed her and said gently:

"My dear mother, breakfast is ready. Come on, get out of bed."

Then she woke up Adhraa and Omar, and the whole family gathered at the breakfast table. Then the conversation began to move between them until Adhraa asked curiously:

"Nahla, what do you intend to do? What is your decision?"

Nahla raised her eyebrows and looked at her, surprised by the question, as if Adhraa did not know that she was an employee now and was on annual leave.

She smiled and said calmly,:

"My dear Adhraa, I'm here on a visit. I have three weeks of annual leave, and then I will return to work."

But Adhraa responded with some tension:

"I know you came to visit, but haven't you changed your mind yet? Haven't you seen my mother? She needs everyone close to her."

Nahla's response was decisive:

"Mom is in my heart and with me wherever I am. I spoke with Omar to start the visa procedures for her to visit me in Canada. I hope she agrees so I can take care of her there."

Their mother was surprised and said:

"For God's sake, Nahla, how can I live away from my children? Nadine and Jumana will come to visit us in four days, and so will Marwan. I never leave my house."

Nahla smiled and replied confidently and calmly:

"My dear Mm, I am very happy that you are settled, and all my brothers and sisters are around you, visiting you always, and this is something that reassures my heart. But I did not get married, and I do not have children living there with me. I found myself in Toronto, established my business and my entity there, and I love it. From the first day I set foot on Canadian soil, Omar was my supporter and did not leave me. Like you, I found my kingdom, and I am not prepared to give it up. She was silent for a few moments then she continued:

"Since this topic was brought up on the first day of my visit, I would like to clarify some important matters to my brothers. Please, let us enjoy this family vacation, and then each of us can return home. I would like to clarify an important matter. From this moment, I will not accept any opinion or discussion from any brother or sister on this subject."

Omar intervened with decisive words:

"Nahla has proven herself trustworthy and self-sufficient. She has restructured her life and established an independent entity. My wife,

children, and we are with her, and we will not abandon her. As the older brother, I tell you that Nahla's situation is settled, and she will remain in Canada."

Ayad was unable to find anything to say and simply said one sentence:

"Congratulations on what you are doing, Nahla. May God grant you success and guide your steps."

After breakfast, to break the ice, Omar asked Adhraa for a cup of coffee, and everyone sat in the living room, chatting. Nahla, however, quietly slipped into her room to call her lifelong friend, Alaa. Alaa was surprised by the call and delighted, and invited her to visit her in Sharjah. The visit would take place six days later, so that Howayda could arrive from Riyadh.

(2)
Between The Warmth of Family's The Frost of Distance

Independence does not mean denying family, just as love does not mean violating dignity. Only balance creates peace

Four days after Nahla and Omar arrived at the family home, Jumana, Nadine, and Marwan arrived. That day was like a small holiday in the big house. The siblings hadn't met together for many years, and this was the first time they had all met without the grandchildren.

Their mother sat at the head of the dining table, her face beaming with light and joy as she looked at them with the gaze of a mother who had longed for them. Then she was satisfied. They exchanged laughter and recalled childhood memories and the days of old when they were young, filling the house with noise and laughter.

But, as is usually the case with family gatherings, there was some tension and tension. While the table was laden with colorful food, and everyone was gathered around it, preparing for lunch, Jumana gave her sister Nahla a look that held meaning, hidden expressions, and a touch of curiosity. She asked her in a voice that seemed calm, but which carried within it a provocative tone and a kind of bullying:

"How was your life in Canada, Nahla? Aren't you tired of working in shops and sewing? And where is your university degree? We haven't seen it"

Everyone fell silent, as if the words had cast a shadow of tension over the table. They knew that Jumana didn't ask in vain, and that she wasn't good at hiding her sarcastic tone, but this time she encountered an unusual calm from Nahla. Nahla raised her head and looked into Jumana's eyes with a look of confidence and reassurance, and said in a calm but clear voice:

"I excuse you because you don't know much about life in the West. There, no one depends on his father or sister to support him, because they consider that a kind of begging. They believe in work, effort, and perseverance, and they believe that every hard worker gets a share. I worked in Abu Hilal's shop, yes.

And his daily wage was a support to me, and I never needed some help from others. Sewing was an additional source of income for me, and at the same time, it fulfilled my dream of making a name for myself among the Arab communities, and what I saved before my travel also helped me.

As for my university degree, ask your brother Omar, he attended my graduation ceremony. Most importantly, my current work in the nursing home is not just a job, but a noble humanitarian mission in which I extend a helping hand to people who want to be self-reliant, not wait for sympathy from others.

Silence prevailed for a moment, and Jumana felt embarrassed. Her stubbornness prevented her from responding. However, Nadine did not remain silent. Rather, she found in Nahla's words an opportunity to present a different point of view. She looked at Nahla and said firmly:

"Westerners do not believe in family cohesion, and in our culture, the family does not leave anyone in need. This is not charity or kindness, but love and duty."

Nahla smiled, then replied:

"May God honor you, Nadine. You are the best example of family cohesion, and your siblings' love for you is a testament to that. But love does not mean that a person loses his independence, abandons his dignity, depends on his family, and spends his entire life begging from them."

Omar intervened at the right moment, sensing that the conversation was starting to take an unnatural turn. He said in the voice of a wise father:

"We are all adults, and each of us has our own life and privacy. I believe we should respect Nahla's privacy, and her words are clear. As for sarcasm or hurtful insinuations, they are completely unacceptable."

Everyone fell silent, but the tension remained in the air. Jumana withdrew from the table without saying a word, and Nadine followed her. As usual, Marwan chose silence as a wall between him and any disagreement. His neutral nature ensured that he wouldn't lose Nadine. In the evening, Jumana, Nadine, and Marwan suggested that Ayad or Adhraa take them to the mall to do some shopping. As they were getting ready, Jumana turned to Nahla and asked her in a tone that was somewhat haughty:

"Nahla, would you like to accompany us?" Nahla answered them with a calm smile:

"Thank you, because tomorrow I'm going to Sharjah to meet Alaa and Howaida. I'll spend one night there and then come back to you, so I prefer to stay with my mother."

Suddenly, Jumana exploded, saying:

"So you didn't miss us at all. All you missed was your friends."

She said it loudly, as if she was addressing everyone in the room, trying to incite her mother and Adhraa as well.

But Nahla, with firmness and calm, responded, saying:

"My dear Jumana, I will only be going for one day, and I will spend the night with Alaa. I will leave the atmosphere of home and family to you, and I hope you all have a wonderful time."

Then she stood up quietly and entered her room, closing the door behind her.

She sat on the edge of the bed and began to prepare her small bag. She wasn't running away, but rather looking for a moment of peace, away from the small conflicts that exhausted her heart. She knew very well that sometimes separation doesn't mean coldness, but rather temporary comfort, a distance that allows hearts to yearn without being hurt. While she was sitting in her room, she heard Jumana inciting Adhraa against her. For the first time, she smiled to herself, and her steps grew more certain and steadier, for she knew that peace sometimes comes from separation, not argument.

Chapter Twenty-One

(1)
Passage to the Self

You may not hold accountable the one who broke us sarcastically, but we heal when we decide not to accompany him again

On a new morning, Nahla woke up before everyone else. She didn't wait for the sound of her siblings' laughter, nor did she want them to gather around the breakfast table.

She got up quietly, as if she didn't want to wake something inside her. She changed her clothes, arranged her small bag, then headed to the kitchen to prepare a light breakfast before heading out. Nadine and Jumana had beaten her to the kitchen, so she greeted them warmly. Nadine responded, her tone seemingly kind, however her inside questioning:

"Why all this rush, Nahla? Wait a little while so we can have breakfast together, and then we'll go with you to Sharjah. You meet Alaa and

Howaida, and we'll go shopping. we accompany you, and you accompany us."

In an instant, time froze in Nahla's heart, and the words fell upon her ears like a stone falling into a still pond. This wasn't just a passing invitation, but a key to a memory that had been locked for years. The moment took her back to a time when she was merely a "silent companion." How many times has she taken them to the markets? How many times had she carried their bags and pampered their children, while she was excluded from decisions, opinions about their purchases, and even courtesy.

She remembered a particular day when she was accompanying them to the markets. Nadine bought corn for Marwan and Jumana and exchanged laughter with them. When Nahla asked her for one, Nadine looked at her strongly and provocatively and said:

"You owe me ten dirhams. Either you give it to the taxi driver, or I'll buy you corn with it."

Then, Nahla smiled a broken smile and swallowed her dignity silently, but she didn't forget... She didn't forget the looks of mockery and bullying, nor the whispers, nor even the laughter that was never innocent. The scene returned to its reality, so she returned to the present, looked at Nadine with a different eye this time, then said with a calm, cold calm like the morning breeze:

"In my opinion, Ayad should take you, or you can use public transportation, and don't forget to buy the corn and enjoy your time."

The response wasn't harsh; it was clear, frank, and implied a message that needed no explanation. Nadine understood the message, and a moment of awkward silence prevailed. Nahla didn't wait for more words, didn't sit at the table, and didn't want to discuss it with anyone. She carried her bag and left the house with steady steps, as if leaving behind invisible burdens.

She arrived at the bus stop, sat in the seat, and felt something like freedom. For the first time, she wasn't in pain, nor was she angry; rather, she was grateful for her decision. Her phone rang. Alaa was on the line, her voice as affectionate as ever:

"Nahla, when will you arrive?"

She answered, her eyes gazing out the bus window, watching the long road stretching toward Sharjah:

"I'm on my way, and with every moment I get closer, my longing for you grows. There's only an hour left until I see you."

For the first time, Nahla felt that the road wasn't taking her away from anyone... but rather returning her to herself.

She arrived at the bus stop in Sharjah, where Alaa and Howaida were waiting for her. The meeting was charged with mixed feelings of joy, tears, and hugs, as if time had not passed, as if three and a half years of separation gone in a single moment.

The friends went to Alaa's house. It was noon. For the first time, Alaa didn't cook the food herself, as she always did. Instead, she ordered Nahla's favorite dish from the Iraqi restaurant: Iraqi kebab, which she loves passionately. After lunch, they sat in the living room sipping tea, exchanging gifts and warm words, filled with indescribable happiness.

In the midst of these intimate moments, Alaa called their friend Maha, who lives in Canada. She joined them on the phone, and their conversations, experiences, and memories continued until they didn't realize the time had passed. It was almost sunset without them noticing. At that point, Alaa decided to take Nahla and Howaida to Al Majaz, specifically to Khalid Lake, where the atmosphere was enchanting and the music of the dancing fountain was playing. The night breeze was soft, and they exchanged news and small and big details that they had missed during the years of absence.

Then Howayda asked the question that had been on her mind since the moment Nahla arrived:

"Nahla, please tell me, what were your mother's feelings when you met her? And most importantly... your sisters and brothers? I think the meeting wasn't natural."

Nahla laughed out loud, a laugh that carried many meanings, and said:

"Oh, Howayda... If only you knew how the meeting was. It was hours of love and tenderness, as if they were trying to shorten the time. Jumana and Nadine knew I would be leaving in a few days, so they began their usual movements, activities, and provocations. Time was very tight for them. But thank God, Omar is with me, and my mother has become convinced that it is better for me to be close to my brother Omar in Canada, even if Adhra, Ayad, and Marwan do not share this opinion."

Alaa interrupted her with a sharp comment stemming from old surprise:

"Nahla, trust me, I still haven't found a logical explanation for Jumana and Nadine's hatred of you. They own everything: the house, the children, the grandchildren, and yet, it's as if they are looking for something in you to take away. I often ask myself, is it a psychological disorder? Or is there a deeper reason that we don't know about?"

As if Alaa had put her hand on the wound, Nahla responded calmly:

"I don't have psychological explanations, but I know what I experienced. Jumana loves control and domination and took advantage of Adhra's love for her children because Adhra had not given birth, and she also took advantage of boundless mom's emotion.

My boundless mother, Jumana, always asks for more than she needs, and takes even without asking, with cunning intelligence and sympathy.

However, glory be to God, she did not find blessing in what she took, because she did not ask sincerely. As for Nadine, despite her malice, I see her as poor. Inside she is convinced that everyone is approaching her for money, and that is why she silences them with money to gain their affection. But she forgot that everything can be bought with money... except love."

Howayda said:

"And you never fell short with them. From the little you earned, you gave them, cared for them, and served them. I do not consider serving your brothers a bad thing; rather, I see it as a duty that demonstrates the family's closeness and solidarity. But frankly, what happened to you was not cooperation, but exploitation, to which hatred and bullying was added."

Nahla sighed a long, deep sigh, then said:

"Praise be to God, who led me to steps I never imagined. I heard a lot of criticism: How could you leave your family and distance yourself from them at this age? Society is unforgiving, and these things are not part of our customs and traditions. But I overcame that criticism because I am convinced that I am committed to my boundaries with God, my conscience, myself, and most importantly... my brother Omar lives beside me, and that alone is enough to silence the mouths of the instigators.'

Alaa noticed Nahla's sudden change in expression, so she gently changed the subject and said with a smile:

"What would you like to drink now?"

The response came in one voice, full of laughter:

"Karak tea."

The evening continued with laughter, words, and funny, unforgettable old situations. When they returned to Alaa's house, they were tired and exhausted. Minutes passed until they all fell asleep, their souls filled with warmth, longing, and sincere friendship.

(2)
A Bag of Life… and a Heart That Never Departs.

The meeting is not to see you, but to meet where we have always been… in the heart, despite the distance, and despite the absence

The next morning, the friends woke up early, and over breakfast, Nahla suggested they take her to the market to buy abaya fabrics. Sharjah's markets are famous for their quality and reasonable prices, and for her, it was an irreplaceable opportunity. At the same time, Howayda remembered that she needed to visit the gold souk to buy a wedding gift for her son, while Alaa's only wish was to go to the salon to give herself a few moments of rest after a long day of emotions and travel.

The three friends agreed to spend their day carrying out these tasks. They moved between the markets and the salon, full of camaraderie and laughter, until the day ended and they had accomplished everything they wanted.

As sunset approached, the moment of farewell awaited at the bus stop, where Nahla would depart back to Abu Dhabi. Alaa approached Nahla, looked into her eyes for a long time, and said in a voice full of confidence and longing:

"Nahla, I don't know why this time I didn't shed tears over your absence. Rather, I feel an inner joy, as if you were still with me, and as if my heart is reassured that your comfort is now there, in Canada."

Howaida smiled and added eagerly:

"Indeed… I am very happy about this meeting, and I am certain that we will meet soon. But I hope that your next destination will be Riyadh, and that you come with Alaa to perform Umrah together. It will be the trip of a lifetime, Nahla."

The thought lit up their faces, and they all agreed that the next vacation would be in Riyadh, where hearts meet and souls are purified.

They hugged each other warmly and bid Nahla farewell with love and whispered sincere prayers for happiness and success. As for Nahla, she boarded the bus with indescribable feelings: overwhelming relief, deep reassurance, and inner joy that was about to overflow, but she hid it as usual, as her joy was always for her alone.

She arrived in Abu Dhabi in the evening, and when she entered the family home, she found everyone gathered. Some faces were sullen, while others welcomed her arrival with a cold welcome, filled with scattered warmth.

Omar took the initiative to ask, smiling:

"Tell me, sweetheart, how was the trip? How did things go with you and your lifelong friends?"

She answered him in a calm tone:

"Praise be to God, as if we had never been apart. We had a lot of fun, went shopping, and I said goodbye, hoping to meet again soon."

At that moment, Jumana's gaze did not leave the bags Nahla was carrying, and she asked in a tone not devoid of observation:

"What are these bags? Gifts or your purchases?"

Nahla answered confidently, her tone as firm as it was calm:

"I bought fabrics to sew cloaks. I can't find this kind in Canada, and thank God Omar didn't carry a lot of weight, and he will help me carry it.

Omar laughed in his light way and said, teasingly: "As you wish sweetheart."

Nahla smiled gently and excused herself to her room, exhausted from fatigue. She wanted to rest her body and calmly recall the details of a day charged with emotions and encounters. When she entered the room and closed the door, she neither cried nor laughed. She simply opened her notebook and wrote:

"Today I learned that my heart doesn't need permission to

celebrate, and that happiness is not a destination we reach, but a moment we live sincerely and hide with from eyes that do not understand us. Meeting Alaa and Howaida brought back to me a part of me that I thought was lost. As for the farewell, it wasn't a farewell, but a postponed promise for a soon meeting. I looked into Jumana's eyes and was convinced then. Why should I choose my silence when she accompanies me or is in my life? Praise be to God who taught me how to love silently, walk in peace, and rejoice alone."

Then she closed the notebook and smiled. She had begun to learn... how to love herself as she deserves.

The weeks passed quickly, and the time came to leave, but this time the taste of departure was different. The whole family was present to bid farewell to Nahla and Omar. On the last night before the departure, Nahla sat alone with her mother. She threw herself into her arms, and this time she didn't shed any tears. There was something inside her telling her:

"This is not your place... your place is over there."

As her mother ran her hand through her hair, she whispered to her, saying:

'Nahla, you will travel tomorrow, God willing, but I have a small request before you leave. Do you agree?'

Nahla raised her head in surprise and said calmly, 'Yes, Mom, if I can, I will do it.'

Her mother was silent for a moment, then said:

"I want you to leave while everyone is satisfied with you, and I am the first of them. If you can, go to Marwan, Jumana, and Nadine, kiss them, and apologize to them if you offended them. After all, they are older than you."

Nahla tensed, but she held herself together. She didn't want to leave the house amidst shouting or arguments. However, she felt that her mother was still siding with her sisters, as she always had. She looked into her mother's face and said calmly:

"Mom, there is nothing between me and any of my brothers. As for me, I have not wronged anyone, and they are all my brothers. I hope that the last few hours pass peacefully. Just say goodbye to me as you say goodbye to Nadine, Jumana, and Marwan when they return to their families after the visit. If you can, that is fine, and if you cannot, do not let the last moment be a reason for me to become tense and regret coming to you and visiting you."

Her mother understood that the matter was settled, so she hugged her and said:

"No, my love, I don't want any quarrels. I wish you a successful flight, and may God keep you safe."

She kissed her mother and went to her room to sleep. At dawn, Marwan's voice woke her up, calling her to get ready to go to the airport. She got up quickly as if she was racing to reach her destination. Everyone was awake.

Adhraa offered them breakfast, but Nahla quickly replied: "We don't have much time; we'll have breakfast at the airport."

Everyone said goodbye to Nahla and Omar with kisses and hugs, and then Ayad drove them to Abu Dhabi Airport, wishing them a successful flight.

When the plane door closed, Nahla felt like she had become a new person.

Full of energy and freedom. She broke the shackles that bound her for years, and now she was beginning a new journey, marked by hope. In a moment of clarity within herself, Nahla opened her notebook and wrote: "I leave behind everything that bound me, not out of hatred... but out of love for what I deserve. To a place where I am not asked to justify my heart, or explain my pain, I walk lightly, to begin a life that resembles me."

Chapter Twenty-Two

(1)
Back to Work

In faraway lands, people become homelands, a kind word a roof, and kindness doors that open without keys

Nahla and Omar arrived in Mississauga, where they were received by Omar's wife and children. For the first time, Nahla felt that her feet were firmly planted on Canadian soil. After staying at Omar's house for two days, she had to return to her residence. Omar and his wife drove her to her residence in Toronto, as it was time for her to prepare to return to work after a three-week vacation.

Upon her arrival, she called her friend Maha, who was very happy to hear her voice, and told her that she was coming to see her, and after an hour, they met, There was an endless conversation between them.

At the height of their conversation, Laura, the owner of the house, entered. After greeting them and asking about the trip, Nahla presented Laura with a gift of Iraqi sweets. Laura received her with love and gratitude, then sadly informed her that she was selling the house and moving with her husband and daughter to Vancouver, where her children lived. Nahla and Maha were surprised by this news, so Nahla asked:

"How long do I have to start looking for a place to live?" Laura answered:

"You have three months."

Then she said goodbye and left. Thoughts began to race through Maha and Nahla's minds. Nahla didn't want to leave the house; she loved its proximity to the lake and the forest, and the tranquility and beauty of the place. It was also close to work, and she had made friends and familiarity with the neighbors there. Maha tried to reassure her, telling her that she had plenty of time and that finding a new place to live would not be difficult.

The next morning, Nahla woke up early. Despite the sadness caused by the news of the move, she longed for the forest and the lake. She prepared her breakfast and headed to the forest to enjoy its magical atmosphere. An hour later, she went to work at the elderly care center, as she missed Isabel and her colleagues.

Isabel was very happy about Nahla's return, and her happiness was even greater when Nahla presented her with a gift from Iraq: "Manna Wal Salwa" sweets and a beautiful antique she had bought from a bazaar. They talked and laughed together, and at that moment, Nahla felt that the challenges ahead of her could be overcome, as long as she had friends and warm memories in her life.

While Nahla was talking to Isabel, the latter noticed something different in her features and asked her with concern and tenderness:

"I see you, my dear, not like yourself. Are you suffering from something? Are you sick?"

Nahla smiled kindly and said reassuringly:

On the contrary, praise be to God, my health is good, and my spirits are high after my visit to my family. But yesterday, after I returned to the residence, the owner of the house told me that she was selling it and that I had to leave within three months because she was moving to Vancouver."

Isabel was moved by her words, and extended her hand towards her and said:

"Don't be sad, my dear. We still have enough time to find you a suitable place to live."

Nahla nodded gratefully and said with a reassuring smile:

"Don't worry, I have enough time, and I will find a place that suits me, God willing."

More than two weeks passed, during which Nahla focused on her work and, at the same time, read newspapers and magazines, asking here and there about suitable housing, but to no avail. One day, while she was engrossed in her work, Isabel called her, a look of clear joy on her face.

Nahla asked her in surprise:

"What makes you so happy?"

Isabel answered, almost flying with joy:

"I found you a beautiful place to live. Here, close to work, it's true. It doesn't overlook the forest, but it does face a wonderful lake. The house is large, and its owner had divided it into three apartments, one consisting of a room, a living room, a kitchen, and a bathroom, with a balcony overlooking the front street, and directly in front of it, a lake."

Nahla was very happy, but her joy was not without hesitation, so she said hesitantly:

"Perhaps the rent is high and doesn't suit my income."

Isabel smiled and said:

"Take the address, and go with Maha to see the apartment tomorrow, and then you can decide."

In the evening, upon returning to the residence, Nahla called Maha and told her what had happened. They agreed to visit the apartment the next morning.

Nahla also called her brother Omar and informed him of the situation. He said to her:

"Don't rush. Go see the apartment, but don't sign papers until I see you."

The next morning, Nahla and Maha headed to the apartment address. As soon as she arrived, she felt a strange inner attraction, as if this place belonged to her. The first thing her eyes caught was the reflection of the sun's rays on the surface of the lake. The water was so clear that she saw the shadows of the trees as if they were a painting hanging in a mirror. She stood for a few minutes, captivated by the scene, before Maha reminded her:

"Let's see the apartment from inside."

They knocked on the door, and a man in his seventies with gray hair, sharp eyes and a serious face opened it. He welcomed them and invited them in, accompanied by his wife. When he opened the door of the apartment, Nahla felt as if her heart had opened with him. The living room was rather spacious, connected to a balcony overlooking the lake directly. The bedroom was small, but sufficient, and it had a closet Built-in wardrobe.

The kitchen is simple and equipped, and it includes a washing machine, while the bathroom is small but tidy and clean.

Nahla was very impressed with the apartment, especially since its location was only half an hour away from her work by bus, and close to Maha's house, only twenty minutes apart. But she was still worried about the rent. She asked the landlord about the price, but he answered her with a smile:

"Didn't Isabel tell you who I am?" She answered in surprise:

"No, she didn't mention anything."

He and his wife laughed, and he said:

"I am Isabel's brother. When my sister learned that I was renting one of the apartments, she asked me to allocate it to you and to take you into consideration regarding the price."

Nahla's eyes filled with tears from being deeply moved, and after a moment of silence she said:

"I thank you for your generosity. You are truly wonderful, but I can't pay less than the apartment is worth. Just tell me the price, and I'll manage.:

His wife laughed and said kindly:

"Don't worry, we don't rent for money. The house is big, and our children have left for their own lives, so we decided to take advantage of the empty space and have people we trust live with us."

Nahla and Maha smiled with obvious joy, and the man said:

"My name is Jack, and this is my wife, Diana. I am a retired engineer.

Welcome to your new home. As for the rent, you will pay the same as you did in your previous residence. If you want to increase the amount, that is up to you."

Nahla responded gratefully:

"I thank you from the bottom of my heart for this generosity."

She said goodbye to them and went to work, her heart brimming with joy. As soon as she saw Isabelle, she hugged and kissed her and said:

"Thank you from the bottom of my heart for the wonderful apartment, and your brother and his even more wonderful wife."

That evening, Nahla called Omar and told him. He was very happy and told her, "Tomorrow morning I will be with you and we will go to the apartment so I can meet the landlord and sign the contract, and I will be your sponsor." Nahla was very happy, and before she went to sleep, she opened her notebook and wrote,

"There are places we do not choose, but they choose us and whisper to us: You belong here."

(2)
My Kingdom... Even If it Were Simple

A month had passed since she met Jack and Diana, and with it, a new chapter in Nahla's life had begun. She moved into her new apartment, which she liked to call "my little kingdom." Her joy was indescribable, not only because she had found a place that suited her, but also because she had chosen it herself and made it with her own hands. At the end of every week, she would go out with Maha to used furniture stores, sifting through the pieces as if searching for treasure. She wasn't looking for something new, but rather something with a soul, something similar to herself. She viewed every old piece of furniture with an eye for art, calling it "antique," and smiling as if she had discovered a piece of history.

Through her acquaintance with the Arab community, she learned of a skilled upholsterer who brought old sofas back to life. She bought a set of sofas and a wooden dining table with four chairs. They were in poor condition, but she saw them as sleeping beauty. She sent them to the upholster and eagerly awaited the results.

When the pieces were returned after their restoration, she couldn't believe her eyes... They were as good as new, even more beautiful than before. She saw in them the spirit of the past and the softness of the present.

She chose a metal bed that needed some repair, so the same upholsterer repaired it for her. She made sure to buy a new mattress, keen on cleanliness and peace of mind. On the day of the move, her brother and his wife came to help her. When they entered the apartment, the couple were surprised by the beauty of the place and the fine taste in arranging the furniture and colors. Everything indicated that this apartment was not just a residence, but a home, with a soul and a story.

The balcony was the most beautiful detail, overlooking the lake with its deep tranquility, embracing the sun every morning, and the birds singing by her window. Nahla stood there looking, breathing, and feeling for the first time since arriving in Canada, that she was at home. In one corner of the living room, she created a small space for sewing, her old hobby that took her to another world. She placed the sewing machine on a simple table, next to a small cupboard containing all her sewing tools and supplies. The corner resembled an artist's studio, filled with order, warmth, and inspiration. And so, with calm, determination, and love, Nahla built her own kingdom.

On the evening of the first day Nahla spent the night in her new apartment, she sat on the couch, opened her notebook, and wrote:

"My dear Nidal... Since you left my life physically, your soul has been and still is with me. I have been dreaming of the home that I could live in. But I did not strive to have a home, and I did not think of looking for one, because I knew I was a guest, even when I lived with my family. I did not have anything special. I was always looking for a corner where my heart could rest...

And here I am today, building it... with a piece of furniture, a memory, a cup of tea on the balcony. In this exile, I did not suddenly find myself, but rather I gathered it piece by piece, just as I gathered the furniture of my apartment, with spirit, patience, and taste."

She closed her notebook and rested her head on the sofa. She didn't cry or smile, she just felt something like serenity. Perhaps because she acknowledged the truth that she was a guest at everything. And because today, with her small hand, she hung the curtain of her little kingdom, and with her patience chose every detail in her apartment, to give things their meaning, Nidal is gone. Yes. And his spirit will continue to flutter around me... and life goes on... for a more beautiful tomorrow full of reassurance.

She looked out at the balcony and whispered:

"I'm here. And this time, I won't leave myself."

Then she turned off the light and went into her room... so that the house began to breathe with her, for the first time... and she said to herself:

"Life didn't give me everything I wished for, but it did give me small corners that I loved more than I dreamed."

The End.

About the Author

Samar Abdulkhalq Al-Samaraïy is an Iraqi author and journalist, born in the Al-Adhamiya district of Baghdad. She is a member of the Iraqi Writers' & Authors' Union and currently resides in Canada.

Her literary journey reflects both her personal experiences and the wider human condition. Through a lyrical and intimate style, Samar bridges memory and imagination, weaving stories that explore identity, belonging, suffering, and renewal.

She is the author of several books:

- Lālie' Omri: Memoirs of a Woman with Multiple Sclerosis (لآلئ عمري) — her debut, a deeply personal memoir of resilience and struggle.
- Ẓilāl al-Ghārdīniya (ظلال الغاردينيا) — published in 2014, a work of fiction exploring human emotion and the shadows of memory.
- Bouh al-Khuzāmā (بوح الخزامى) — a reflective book on life's journey, written with tenderness and poetic depth.

With When the Soul Shines, Samar continues her exploration of the intersections between the personal and the universal, offering readers a story of hope, endurance, and the timeless search for freedom.

www.ingramcontent.com/pod-product-compliance
Lightning Source LLC
Chambersburg PA
CBHW061231070526
44584CB00030B/4069